PATRICK RODEN PHD CAPS

Marketing Your Aging in Place CAPS Business

Copyright © 2024 by Patrick Roden PhD CAPS

All rights reserved. No part of this publication may be reproduced, stored or transmitted in any form or by any means, electronic, mechanical, photocopying, recording, scanning, or otherwise without written permission from the publisher. It is illegal to copy this book, post it to a website, or distribute it by any other means without permission.

Patrick Roden PhD CAPS asserts the moral right to be identified as the author of this work.

Patrick Roden PhD CAPS has no responsibility for the persistence or accuracy of URLs for external or third-party Internet Websites referred to in this publication and does not guarantee that any content on such Websites is, or will remain, accurate or appropriate.

Designations used by companies to distinguish their products are often claimed as trademarks. All brand names and product names used in this book and on its cover are trade names, service marks, trademarks and registered trademarks of their respective owners. The publishers and the book are not associated with any product or vendor mentioned in this book.

None of the companies referenced within the book have endorsed the book.

First edition

Contents

Prologue 1

Introduction 3

1. This I Believe 4
2. Be an Aging in Place Contrarian 19
3. Aging in Place The Opportunity 39
4. Rethinking Aging in Place "Truisms" 52
5. Introducing Choice Architecture and PhotoVoice 72
6. Planning Fallacy and the Consumer Decision Model 88
7. Design Matters 107
8. Your Ideal Client 121
9. Thoughts, Terms, and Tools 133
10. Conclusion 154

Epilogue 155

About the Author 156

Also, by Patrick Roden PhD CAPS 157

Prologue

When I first envisioned this book, I was drawn to the title *Beyond Ramps and Rails* (I kept the title simpler). It would have perfectly encapsulated the broader scope of this work: an exploration of what it truly means to serve as an Aging in Place Professional (AIPP). While the built environment—ramps, grab bars, and thoughtful remodeling—is vital, the heart of this mission goes far beyond construction. It's about understanding the lives you're transforming and the trust you're building with every project.

The objective has always been clear: to help you stand out, not just as a skilled contractor-remodeler, but as an empathetic advocate and expert in aging-in-place solutions. By applying the strategies and insights shared here, you can elevate your business and your impact, creating a legacy of care and excellence that outshines the competition.

Remember, you're not just remodeling homes—you're creating spaces where people can continue to live their best lives, with dignity and Inter-independence. Thank you for committing to this important work and may your journey as an AIPP continue to inspire, empower, and set the standard for this vital industry.

This is an exciting time to be an Aging in Place Professional. The demographic wave of aging adults—expected to reach 80.8 million by 2040, according to the U.S. Census Bureau—creates an unprecedented opportunity in a market projected to hit $2 trillion by 2032. You are undeniably in the right place at the right time.

But abundance doesn't guarantee success. My goal is to help you become **best in class**. By applying the ideas and strategies in this book, you will establish a powerful differentiator—one that sets you apart in an industry brimming with potential. The result? A steady stream of referrals as word-of-mouth builds your reputation as a trusted expert in aging-in-place solutions. Unlike spending hours chasing clients through advertising or social media, this approach allows you to focus on what truly matters: your craft and your clients.

I promise I've given you my best ideas and actionable strategies. The rest is up to you. When you succeed, you'll not only grow your business but scale this mission of helping people stay in the comfort and safety of their homes by choice. What you do matters profoundly. Let that purpose fuel your journey and amplify your impact.

Introduction

I decided to write a book designed for CAPS Aging in Place Professionals (AIPPs). The motivating reason is because for decades now I have been studying, thinking, reading, writing, giving talks, doing interviews, and working in the field of aging- in-place, and it's time to share some useful ideas (secret sauce) in one place.

I have earned some key insights about aging in place over the years that are contrarian, maybe even controversial, and I want to put them all in one accessible format for the professionals in the field, and those just starting out. There are multiple conventional wisdoms that deserve shaking up. As well as a few new market possibilities on the horizon to explore, business techniques to try, and some guiding theories to consider.

My goal is to share tips, theory, techniques, and some surprises that I've learned along the way.

I feel compelled to do more than just post on social media about these concepts as an intellectual exercise—and never see them make positive changes in real lives. My purpose is to scale the ideas through you and help with your success.

My sincerest goal is for all who read this book to embrace the philosophy that human development is possible all along the life course. In your heart you must believe what you do matters and provided the right interventions, older adults are fully capable of remaining home by choice. I hope after sharing the ideas in this work, you will embrace some as guiding principles in your business and in the lives of those you touch.

Do good while you're doing well, to your success, Patrick

What You Do Matters.

1

This I Believe

What is "Aging in Place?"

Let's establish what Aging in Place is before we get too far into this.

National Association of Home Builders: Aging in place means remaining in one's home safely, independently, and comfortably, regardless of age, income, or ability level. It means the pleasure of living in a familiar environment throughout one's maturing years, and the ability to enjoy the familiar daily rituals and the special events that enrich all our lives. It means the reassurance of being able to call a house a "home" for a lifetime.

The CDC Definition: The ability to live in one's own home and community safely, independently, and comfortably, regardless of age, income, or ability level.

Author's (my) Long Definition: Aging in place is much more than being in an environment of choice as one gets older, it means home – a place where emotional and functional needs are met. Home is a foundation where family histories are created, and rich memories have been woven from shared experiences. Home contains a lifetime of cherished objects that support identity and delight the senses. It's also nestled in the community that's been cultivated over the years, which is the center of those daily rituals that are loved so much.

Many plan to stay; it's where they *live*—and you, the Aging- in-Place CAPS Professional can make that possible.

Next let's establish why is having personal philosophy important As a CAPS Professional?

A personal philosophy defines who you are and what you stand for.

It's your identity.

Think of great humanitarians, Mother Teresa, Gandhi and Martin Luther King all had doctrines by which they lived. These beliefs gave them direction and purpose. Everything they did was because of these values.

Too many of us settle for lives without any sense of purpose and thus lack fulfillment.

We live aimlessly, day to day without any intention. But this shouldn't be. With a personal philosophy, we will be able to live with purpose and create daily intentions that serve as a roadmap for life.

If you were to plan a trip and left the house without directions, you wouldn't reach your destination. A personal philosophy is your directions. Use it to reach the destination of fulfillment.

Source: medium.com

Aging in Place

It may seem strange to start with a personal philosophy in a book about your aging-in-place business but trust me you need a strong foundation to build on and you'll see why later.

I have invested many hours contemplating this simple yet meaningful 3-legged stool on which I think about aging in place. Sharing it up front serves two purposes:

1. You know where I stand
2. You will take the time to formulate your own.

I believe 3 things about aging in place:

1) Shelter is at the core of what it means to be human.

2) As Laura L. Carstensen, Ph.D., Founding Director of the Stanford Center on Longevity, noted: *"Our environments presume youth,"* therefore adaptation is required.

3) Aging-in-place is an Ecosystem, a network of interactions between living beings and their environment controlled by internal factors (mind/body) and external factors (society, built

environment, financial, support systems, and technology)–thus, to be more independent you're going to have to be more INTER-dependent.

Why start here, you may still be asking? Because you can't shoot a cannon out of a canoe. Allow me to explain, you need a strong foundation to work from while making your difference in the world. Think of it as a theoretical aircraft carrier on which you will take off and land throughout your career. Successful people have a personal philosophy that acts as a guidepost, true north in their lives.

Most successful people have at least one guiding principle: phrases or ideas by which they live and work. These keep you focused. They help you make decisions. They inspire you—or ground you. Steve Jobs was known for his many principles for a successful career and life, but most of them revolve around positivity, looking toward the future, and not being afraid to fail forward.

Source: themuse.com

I have opened with my personal philosophy concerning aging- in-place and encourage you to borrow elements, adopt it, or create your own. Steve Jobs was about "making a dent in the world," if a personal/business philosophy served him well, it will do the same for you. Just do it (thank you Nike).

Since we are on this journey together, I wanted you to know my Aging in Place Manifesto right from the start. These three concepts will be the scaffolding on which the ideas shared in this book will be based.

Let's briefly unpack each to give you a better feel for how they will influence your thinking and in turn, your work and bottom line.

Idea #1

Shelter is at the core of what it means to be human.

My dear aging-in-place professional (AIPP), always remember that what you do matters—more than you will ever know. Read that again.

Over the years working in ICU as a nurse, I was privileged to witness the most tender of moments between couples. When the life of a loved one is threatened it brings out deepest emotions of what it means to be human.

Many times, I watched bedside vigils that only love could explain. I write on the topic of aging in place and living in environments of choice as we all get older because it is important; shelter is at the core of what it means to be human. We all need a safe physical dwelling in which to situate our lives and cultivate meaning—and here is no higher human

undertaking than to love and be loved in return.

Home is often the setting in which this meaning-making occurs. In my experience most patients had two desires: first for a healing and restored wellness, then without exception, to go Home...

Idea #2

Our environments presume youth.

In four words Laura L. Carstensen, Ph.D., Founding Director of the Stanford Center on Longevity nailed it. This in my opinion is the single most profound statement ever made on the topic of aging in place. So, it follows that adaptation is required.

It is not news to you that many older adults prefer aging in place, remaining in their current homes or communities. Most seniors are already aging in place in traditional communities. These communities were built for young 6 foot tall 190-pound healthy GIs returning home from WWII with young families. The communities were built largely to accommodate these growing families: Detached single-family houses; large lots; cheap land; accessible by highways; isolated from commerce and traffic.

What the developers of the 1950s didn't anticipate was the rejection of the Suncity model of retiring to age-segregated societies in the desert south by future generations. The unin- tended consequences of baby boomers staying put was the first Suburban Generation aging in place.

The young children of the WWII generation who grew up in suburbia, the baby boomers (1946-1964) by 2030 will all be 65 or older. And most of this demographic transition has occurred in the suburbs. In fact, according to the U.S. Census Bureau, as of 2020, approximately 51% of baby boomers lived in suburban areas.

What was once favored for its "get-away" location from big city metropolis and hassles, now has the potential to be a disaster for aging boomers. The suburbs have been termed "the architecture of isolation" by age-friendly city planners for the very same reasons they were appealing to young GIs raising families. Up front is the location–it's auto-dependent, next is the built environment–it's youth-dependent. Both conditions are BIG problems offshore brewing for aging boomers (especially women) who are staying put.

These homes/neighborhoods are what Jon Pyoons, Ph.D., Professor at USC Davis School of Gerontology calls "Peter Pan Housing." The term describes housing for people who think they are never going to get old. Pyoons notes:

"We have narrow hallways, slippery bathrooms, and houses are crammed full of stuff."

15 Elements of a Peter Pan House

1) Multi-level housing
2) Miles from a bus stop or light-rail transient
3) No markets within walking distance many miles away (auto-dependent)
4) Medical care out of reach
5) Neighborhood Lacks sidewalks
6) Large hills and sloping yards
7) Porch-less
8) Steps to enter the home
9) 24-inch doorways
10) Rural Isolation
11) Washer/Dryer downstairs

12) Bathroom upstairs

13) HIGH-MAINTENANCE lawn/exterior

14) Older Housing Stock

15) Clutter

After WWII young families flocked to the suburbs to live the American dream and are now senior citizens facing challenges with their living situations. The challenge with the new developments is much like the ones facing the old developments; these are auto-oriented living areas which require commuter trips due to the geographic isolation. The construction was designed for young-able-bodied adults, and many aren't pedestrian friendly for older people and lack civic or shopping centers.

CAPS Chat TIP

If you want a BIG opprotyunity find a BIG Problem—aging in place is both.

~ Patrick Roden PhD CAPS

So, it is a bad news/good news scenario; the bad news is aging in homes designed for youth are the norm. The United States is home to a large population of both elderly and disabled people, but only 10% of housing across the country is "age- ready" and equipped with features that make them accessible to such individuals (forbes.com). This was one of the takeaways recently from Laying the Foundation: Housing Accessibility and Affordability for Older Adults and People with Disabilities, a hearing held by the U.S. Senate's Special Committee on Aging.

Idea #3

Aging-in-place is an Ecosystem

I have always advocated for discussing aging in place in context, that is the concept is contextual and can only be viewed in relation to other factors than just the built environment. In other words, to fully understand aging in place and therefore make it work, you must be aware of the other factors beyond the obvious built environment (ramps/rails).

The lens through which to approach this is called "systems thinking." Systems thinking is a way of understanding how things are connected and work together as a whole, rather than just focusing on individual parts. It helps us see the bigger picture and recognize that changes in one part of a system can affect other parts. Think of it like looking at the whole forest instead of just focusing on one tree.

Systems thinking is also a diagnostic tool. As in the medical field, effective treatment follows thorough diagnosis. In this sense, systems thinking is a disciplined approach for examining problems more completely and accurately before acting. It allows us to ask better questions before jumping to conclusions. Systems thinking often involves moving from observing events or data, to identifying patterns of behavior over time, to surfacing the underlying structures that drive those events and patterns. By understanding and changing structures that are not serving us well (including our mental models and perceptions), we can expand the choices available to us and create more satisfying, long-term solutions to chronic problems.

In general, a systems thinking perspective requires curiosity, clarity, compassion, choice, and courage. This approach includes the willingness to see a situation more fully, to recognize that we are interrelated, to acknowledge that there are often multiple interventions to a problem, and to champion interventions that may not be popular (thesystemsthinker.com).

Let's unpack the elements of the Aging in Place Ecosystem. When I use the term "ecosystem" it implies a dynamic balance between the individual/s and the surrounding environment. For healthy functioning and sustainability, an ecosystem's living members must be in balance (interaction) with the non-living elements.

So, to say a network of interactions between living beings and their environment controlled by internal factors (mind/body) and external factors (built environment, financial, support systems, and technology) I am describing two basic entities

1) the person 2) their support system.

CAPS Chat TIP

Aging in Place is a team sport, not about "independence" but rather "Inter-dependence."

~ Patrick Roden PhD CAPS

When taking care of patients, I am aware of the patient in relation to the network supporting them—the context. The same is true for the individual/s aging in place and could be considered aging in place within context.

Let me provide a real-life scenario to show how systems thinking can solve an aging in place challenge. Your new clients are an older couple who have been married 40 years. Their daughter calls you in for a home assessment because the husband has been falling lately in the hallway.

Immediately you see the hallway has several gorgeous antique Persian rugs covering the hardwoods. On closer examination you notice the ends are turned up and frayed. You inquire about the rugs and the couple glowingly recount their honeymoon in the far east and how they bought the rugs as a wedding gift to themselves. They have been laying faithfully on those hardwoods for over 40 years and are a reminder of their younger selves.

The wife quietly admits "he's been tripping over them." You as a compassionate and systems thinking CAPS professional understand that these are what environmental psychologist call meaningful objects that create place attachment. They support the couple's identity and delight their senses. But you also know they are a tripping hazard and need to be dealt with.

The non-systems thinker will suggest removing them, not knowing this could also cause a biographical disruption, or a break in self-identity (more on this keep reading). The systems thinking professional will consider the problem in context and look for a better solution.

Suggesting the rugs be displayed on the walls as decorations after explaining the risks-benefits of leaving them on the floors displays an understanding how things are connected and work together as a whole—systems thinking.

It solves the tripping hazard while preserving the integrity of home and meaning making for the aging couple. This kind of systems thinking will set you apart from your competition.

I will share more insights in the following chapters but for now, in summary:

1) Shelter is at the core of what it means to be human (What you do matters)

2) Our environments presume youth and require adaptation (Big opportunity)

3) Aging in place is contextual and requires systems thinking to work (Sets you apart)

Human Development the Entire Lifespan (This I Believe too) Biographical Disruption

It is my belief that older adults are self-directed and capable

of human development the entire lifespan. Having noted this, resistance to change is one of the biggest challenges that CAPS remodelers, in-home care professionals and families will encounter.

At some point in your experience with older relatives or clients you will run into a brick wall when suggesting modifications to their homes. In medicine we call this phenomenon "stasis" or standing still–and so often in life when things cease to move, like blood for example, trouble is just offshore brewing.

A common paradox I love to talk about in aging is that to stay the same (often called continuity of self) change is often required. For example, we've all heard the line: *The more things change the more they stay the same,* in this context I'd like to apply it to home modification for aging in place.

As our clients age there are undeniable physiological changes (the problem of recognizing and admitting change) which make negotiating their homes challenging. Further, many homes weren't built to accommodate aging bodies. Given these two realities of changing physiology and static built environments, it is smart for individuals to consider making home modifications (CHANGES) that will help them (or loved ones) remain (SAME) home—this is the aging-in-place paradox.

But many seniors are reluctant to make changes for various reasons which include fear of change, not wanting the home to look like an intuition or medical, and costs. These are often cited, but infrequently addressed is something called "Biographical Disruption" that might be driving the fear of change.

To unpack this let's look at the definitions of the two words which makeup the concept:

Biographical: Information about a person's life, or details about the life of a person.

Disruption: A break or interruption in the normal course or continuation of some activity, process, etc.

When joined, Biographical-Disruption in an older person means a discontinuity of Self, or a fracture of self-identity caused by environmental change. Self-concepts cultivated over years of living in a preferred environment surrounded by objects that support identity suddenly fracture and now, research has shown that older adults are often unable to adjust to new surroundings because of the deterioration of a brain circuit which plays a critical role in goal-directing learning when too much change is introduced.

The Key is to manage change in ways that integrate the new and old to minimize Biographical-Disruption. The beloved Persian rug on the floor, is a great example of avoiding a biographical disruption. No more fall risk, and now it functions as a lovely wall decoration...Aging in Place WIN-WIN!

With aging comes loss—any seemingly small wins like the rug mean more than you will ever know to your clients.

CAPS Chat TIP

Aging is Living.

~ Patrick Roden PhD CAPS

Outdated Thinking

I've been thinking about a fixed mindset vs. a growth mindset in terms of how one views or talks about aging in general. A fixed mindset from the 20th century views aging in peak and decline terms, a remnant from the mid-late-19th century industrial era. The cultural metaphor was body-as-machine, you have a few good years and then you were worn out going into a steep decline. The medical model was predominant in creating this cultural narrative—which origins, in part, go back to the ancient Greeks, by the way. Pathology (disease) was the focus, what goes wrong

with aging, or senescence was the dominant view.

This decline emphasis left little room for human development or any upside to growing older. It is a shame that today there are still those who seem to embrace gerontophobia (fear of aging). To be stuck in this mindset is counterproductive, ironically to their future selves as well. We are all aging; it is a natural process of change over time.

To dislike the term "aging in place" seems to me to fall under the category of a fixed mindset. Aging is not a sin, and like many "isms" ageism is designed for *othering a group of individuals. This dated thinking doesn't belong in the 21st century.

Gerontophobia of this kind denies human potential throughout the life course. If you know a someone who dislikes the term "aging in place" take a moment to ask them why. What image does the term conjure up? Now ask them honestly why they created that image in their head? Are they working off a 20th century prejudice that they were culturally taught? Could they have just as easily envisioned an alternative vision—a 21st century growth mind set image?

Why would "thriving" or "living" be preferable to "aging?" They are not mutually exclusive. It is a choice, like many ideas we all grew up with and didn't question that are now being challenged, maybe it is time to rethink aging in general, and aging in place specifically.

Cultural assumptions can be challenged, and consciousness raised to a new level and view of aging; it has been done with other "isms."

Hanging on to dated ideas threatens one's relevancy and erodes one's soul.

As an aging in place professional you reject ageism, believe older adults are capable and have the right to remain home by choice.

CAPS Chat TIP

Ageism is Never Good Business.

~ Patrick Roden PhD CAPS

I've concluded chapter 1 with this piece on how home modifications (for aging in place) affect others' lives.

Stories of lives transformed

Several years ago, I posted (with permission) this article

Renovations as Stimulus? Home Modifications Can do so Much More to Transform People's Lives by Phillippa Carnemolla, Senior Research Fellow, School of the Built Environment, University of Technology Sydney. The article essentially was about the Australian government's efforts to stimulate the economy during the COVID-19 pandemic.

The stated purpose of the Morrison government's Home- builder program was to stimulate the economy and create construction jobs during the COVID-19 pandemic. Their research showed home improvements could do much more than just add capital value and a spare room. They also restored or maintained a person's ability to live independently – whether they are older, have a disability, are unwell or have been injured.

Carnemolla states, in other words, these home improvements could transform life for any one of us at some point in our lives. They greatly improve people's well-being and reduce dependence on careers. This affects a great many people – including nearly a million who receive some form of aged care in their own home.

Astonishingly the Australian Bureau of Statistics discovered some unexpected results. The study of 157 people receiving community care found home modifications reduced the overall hours of care they required by 42%.

Their quality of life (measured as health-related quality of life) improved by 40%. By reducing care needs and costs, and increasing independence and well-being, home modifications lead to a multitude of government, community, and personal benefits. These include lowering the risk of COVID-19 transmission that providing and receiving personal care entails.

Further, Carnemolla notes, my research measures how home modifications directly influence the amount of care needed to live, and continue living, at home. The study included 157 Australians aged from 15 to 92 who received community care. Some had arthritis, cancer, or a motorcycle injury. Others were born with a disability. All required care in their home.

Hours of care for participants (most of it unpaid care by family and friends) were compared before and after home modifications. The changes liberated them. Home modifications reduced or eliminated their need for help, restored their confidence in caring for themselves and reduced career stress. As people's confidence grew, they were happier to venture out into the broader community. Importantly, relationships improved. Simple home modifications meant David* no longer had to help his mother shower as she could safely do that herself. His mother was saved from the embarrassment of her son being involved in what is normally a private activity. Instead, they could enjoy each other's company with regular activities like shopping and having afternoon tea together.

Ravi* had a spinal injury because of an accident. He was glad to be back at home but was sleeping in a converted sunroom at street level because he couldn't get to his bedroom upstairs. The only bathroom for showering was a small ensuite, up three stairs. Adding an entry ramp makes a home accessible again. The house was not suitable for a wheelchair, so his wife had to help him get around their home. The effort required to take care of basic daily living activities left them too exhausted to even think about going out.

An accessible bathroom with a hand-held shower was installed, as well as a ramp at the home entrance. Not only was Ravi able to shower independently again, but he and his wife also regained their energy and interest in going out. He attributed home modifications to enabling them to go to the movies and a restaurant for the first time in the three years after the accident.

You, the CAPS professionals, are the ones who can help make all this possible in real people's lives. Please keep in mind that creating accessible environments which can accommodate compromised bodies will assist in healing and return a sense of wholeness that only home can provide.

Home modifications went far beyond economic stimulus for the Australian government, impacting individual citizen's lives in multiple ways:

1) **Liberating** informal caregivers (family and friends).
2) **Decreasing stress** for caregivers and care recipients.
3) **Increasing Self-efficacy** (belief in one's capacity) of home dwellers.
4) **Restoring dignity** and sense of normalcy for all involved. These were unintended positive consequences of home modifications for aging in place accessibility.

Author Note

Disclosure statement: In her capacity as a Senior Research Fellow at UTS, Phillippa Carnemolla has received funding from the National Disability Insurance Agency (NDIA) through their ILC grant program. Phillippa is a Director for the Centre for Universal Design Australia (CUDA) and sits on the City of Sydney Disability (Inclusion) Advisory Panel.

This article was originally published on TheConversation.com Permission given to repost/images Patrick Roden of aginginplace.com

(* *Names have been changed to protect anonymity*)

Finally, I want to thank you for picking up this book. From the outset my goal is for you to succeed in your business goals. For decades I have been reading and writing on the topic of aging in place. I now see it as my mission **to help you be BEST in class** by sharing concepts and ideas that can be a differentiator setting you apart in the field.

With your success, each individual and family you serve will fulfill my dream of helping as many as possible with aging in place. It is through you that I scale my purpose of keeping the dreams of countless older adults and their families alive.

What you do matters.

References

Forbes.com [Aging In Place Statistics And Facts In 2024 – Forbes](Health)

Othering: The act of treating someone as though they are not part of a group and are different in some way.

~ dictionary.cambridge.org

2

Be an Aging in Place Contrarian

I've never walked the same path other people found comfortable and I'm not going to start now.

- Lora Leigh, Forbidden Pleasure

There are three leading paradigms having to do with Aging in Place that are pretty much gospel among the faithful. I have been hearing about them relentlessly over the years and pushed back whenever possible. I will outline them for you providing the conventional wisdom line along with my contrarian take on each.

My goal is for you to be aware of what the "thought leaders" are saying and give you another interpretation so you are informed of both sides.

Point #1

Never use the term "Aging in Place" when marketing

Point #2

Aging in Place vs. Aging in *THE RIGHT* Place

Point #3

Aging in Place is about Independence

———————————-

Point #1

Never use the term "Aging in Place" when marketing

You can't handle the truth!

~Col Jessep A Few Good Men written by Aaron Sorkin

Thriving in Place, Living in Place, anything but aging in place!

What is A Euphemism? Definition by Rich Coffey:

"A euphemism is a substitution of a delicate or inoffensive term or phrase for one that has coarse, sordid, or otherwise unpleasant associations."

We are a culture awash in euphemisms. Day-in-day-out, our large flat screens spoon-feed sugarcoated "facts" that keep us insulated and disconnected from reality. For example, here are a couple we're all familiar with:

Certified pre-owned = USED

Genuine Imitation Leather = Cheap Vinyl

Author George Orwell (Book 1984) called this kind of re- framing doublespeak. Call it what you like, it is deliberately deceptive language and it's everywhere.

Thriving in Place

When I read about a new movement euphemistically called "Thriving in Place" I understood the goal behind the marketing. Gerontophobia (fear of aging) is driving this, and if you want to sell services or products, the smart marketers tell you to avoid the word "aging" like the plague. This falls into the "anti-aging" category and is a veiled form of ageism. It sounds lovely, and something a marketer or politician would say to sell you what they are offering.

Don't get me wrong, many older adults are living full and exciting lives at home (dare I say thriving) and in their com- munities. In my own experience I find living at home lies somewhere on a continuum from so-called "thriving" to low- energy days, and every shade in-between. I'm not unlike most middle-aged and older adults, we simply want a level of "independence" within our community, a space to cultivate our own uniqueness, and to preserve our natural daily rituals and routines (biorhythms/natural flow if you will). This defines *aging in place* for so many.

So please don't market older adults with euphemisms, they are adults who have earned the respect not to be patronized. Sell them on non-stigmatizing design and function that respects aging for what it is, a natural process of development and change.

They can handle the truth...

Marketing Assisted Living

For years now, especially in the Assisted Living industry which has a vested interest in casting shade on the term "aging in place," there has been concerted effort to deny that aging is living. For example, here is an assisted living marketer throwing shade on the concept:

If I were "shopping" on behalf of a parent today, I would be **turned off rather quickly by a community touting aging in place. For me, the term conjures up images of an older person in a rocking chair with a glazed look, an idle stare and cobwebs encircling their frail body. Maybe it's just me, but that's the mental picture "aging** *in place" gives to me. And as they say, "A picture is worth a . . ."* **In truth, I cannot think of a more dour and depressing term.**

~ Mr Thriving* / senior living website

Further, the author has a black and white image of a rocking chair for the image of his article. I don't know this gentleman, at the time of writing he stated he was retired and starting a new gig in the assisted living industry.

My point about Mr. Thriving* is this, he's most likely over 65 himself—yet look at how he describes aging in place! This is a classic case of internalized ageism, and gerontophobia, yet somehow, it's still acceptable to him.

I always frame these arguments and attempts at rebranding "aging in place" as "thriving in place" or living in place" in terms of euphemisms for marketing—follow the money.

Ageism like this from older adults appears to be a veiled form of self-loathing, activist and author, Betty Friedan described it many years ago in Fountain of Age (1993). It is a form of "othering" that separates us from older adults.

Author Margaret Gullette notes: "We are aged more by culture than by chromosomes," and this insidious decline narrative is getting applied earlier to younger people.

A push back on this kind of ageism is needed and positive associations around aging must be normalized. But to embrace this concept our society must change its view of what it means to grow old, and you as an AIPP can help achieve this.

As pointed out in Nortin M. Hadler's book, Rethinking AGING (UNC Press 2011), the secret to longevity is the structure of society, not whether anyone eats bran. It is the social construction that Americans have been taught and nearly all have accepted about aging and its issues, that really matters.

Mr. Thriving*(drank the cool aid) ends with these thoughts: *With the heightened importance of social engagement, an active, vibrant environment — and what memory care guru Dr. John Zeisel, founder and CEO of The Hearthstone Institute calls, "a life worth living" — I can't think of a more counterproductive phrase than "aging in place." Several other baby boomers and adult children I've talked to agree. Some even wince and laugh at the notion — as*

I first did.

For lack of a better alternative, I've started using the term "Living in Place" for some of our client communities. So far, no objections. For me, Living in Place is a more accurate, representative and uplifting option. We're supposed to be about lifestyle and living, right? Why highlight aging?

As they say (rightly or wrongly), "perception is everything" (irony! my comment). Do you want your community known for aging in place or living life to the fullest for as long as you can without ever having to move?

What do you think? Do you aspire to "age in place", or would you prefer to thrive in a comfortable, vibrant community that you never have to leave?

Am I making a big deal over nothing? Is there another term you are currently using? Is it descriptive yet uplifting? I'd love to hear your thoughts on the matter. And thank you for indulging me! Maybe it's just my age . . .

Dear Mr. Thriving* I doubt you're going to love to hear my thoughts, but there they are. I hope you've changed your outlook on the term "aging in place" since posting this article—aging is not a sin!

Summary

I can't emphasize how out of touch this line is: "We're supposed to be about lifestyle and living, right? Why highlight aging?" As if those are mutually exclusive!

To think like an aging in place contrarian USE the term "Aging in Place" not only with colleagues and professional insiders—but especially with clients. Aging is not a four-letter word, respect your client's position in life and don't patronize them with euphemisms. They can handle the truth...

<u>CAPS Chat TIP</u>

Pro-Aging is Good Business

~ Patrick Roden PhD CAPS

Assisted Living Data Points FYI

Average Age of Assisted Living Residents: Around half of assisted living residents in the U.S. are at least 85 years old. Just over 30% of residents are between 75 and 84 years old. About 13% of residents are between 65 and 74 years old. Just 6% of residents are younger than 65 years old.

Aging and the Realities of getting Older (No *Happy Gerontology Here)

Early in my nursing career I remember listening to the lungs of an elderly woman who was admitted with exacerbation of congestive heart failure. She was what we call in the business "a frequent flyer" because of her many admissions for acute episodes of chronic conditions.

As I carefully placed my stethoscope into my ears, then strategically on her chest, I requested that she take: "BIG BREATHS—BIG BREATHS" (in my nurse voice). Suddenly she said something and then began to chuckle with light laughter—not being able to hear, I pulled the ear prong out of one ear and asked her: "What did you say?" Her response has stayed with me some 30 years later...

In a quivering Parkinson-like voice (think Katharine Hepburn in later years): "THEY USED TO BE..." The smirk smile that came over her face added levity to the tense situation, and I laughed out loud!

Through the years I have always told this story as a highlight in my career. It speaks to the truth about aging and how essential it is to be able to accept the realities of growing older and what it brings. If we are fortunate to experience old age (and not all are) hopefully we will be able to have a sense of lightheadedness about the changes–like that woman did. This is beyond making fun of older adults, or ageism, it is about being real.

Bold Ad Campaign Dares to Ask: Do You Want to be an Old Woman?

Kaiser Permanente years ago, had an Ad campaign that was bold and brilliant in that it flies in the face of conventional wisdom in several important ways:

1. We want you to use our services (not a typical insurance model) 2. The 3rd rail in marketing is to mention the word "aging" or "old" you must instead use euphemisms ("Thriving in Place") when selling to boomers. This was golden rule #1 and Gerontophobia is the reason. 3. Traditional medical model privileged sick-care not healthcare. Emphasis on the Peak-and- Decline model of aging. Focus on pathology and what goes wrong.

This campaign had the audacity to ask the question straight out: "DO YOU WANT TO BE AN OLD WOMAN? **"It is NOT about**

ANTI-aging–in fact, just the opposite. Emphasize preventive care (get a mammogram) so you can live long enough to BECOME AN OLD WOMAN! And live all the experiences awaiting you.

When I grow up is a message that demonstrates a deeper understanding of human behavior and respects maturing psyches of older adults who are embracing all ages of their human experience. Living fully within each age is a choice and there is pleasure at every age.

Do not be afraid to talk about "aging in place" show your clients you are not buying into gerontophobia. Keep it real...They will appreciate you for it. Top of Form

Point #2

<u>Aging in Place vs. Aging in *THE RIGHT* Place</u>

Every bad situation is a blues song waiting to happen.

~ Amy Winehouse

I have been a nurse since 1985 (25 of those years in acute/coronary/trauma/Neuro ICU, and post-surgical recovery currently). As well as a nursing home aide before that while I was earning my undergraduate degree. This kind of life experience is a hard–hit- ting reality, and you either learn coping mechanisms–or you find some other line of work.

I have been in the arena, not theoretically, but in the flesh, working with all kinds of people in all kinds of scenarios (many unimaginable to the public). I mention this because I also have invested many years in educational pursuits in the field of aging (gerontology) studying theory. So, I feel uniquely qualified to speak to the notion of "aging in place vs. Aging in the right place." I have some hands-on experience working with older adults and extensive theoretical scaffolding built over decades researching theories. One foot on the ground, one foot in the clouds, if you will.

CAPS Chat Tip

Aging in Place:

A Dynamic Self-determined process of Living at home INTER-dependently as you age.

~ Patrick Roden PhD

Aging in Place by the Numbers

When I read about "aging in *the right* place" the theoretical me thinks *it's pretty to think so* (thank you Earnest Hemmingway). Wouldn't it be lovely if everyone could pull up stakes, leave their un-age-friendly homes and neighborhoods just before the fall. With perfect pre-planning and timing, everyone escapes to sunny greener pastures of 20-minute neighborhoods that are safe, walkable, well lighted, green spaces, shopping, entertainment, no crime, universal design environments, fully accessible homes, and geotechnology smart home infused dwellings, with health clubs and Starbucks on the corner.

As FORBES Health describes: (having all your ducks in an aging-in-place-row)

Aging in place successfully requires careful planning, and often a caregiver, social support system and consideration of potential future health issues, such as heart disease, diabetes and cognitive decline.

Wouldn't it be lovely, making the future a part of one's current philosophy with careful planning. Setting up a social support network ahead of time, caregivers (formal and informal), getting into accessible built environment remodeling before needing it, and having the savings to afford moving or modifications, and in-home care.

Yes, living independently in the perfect setting (the right place) into the sunset...

Those Pesky Reality Numbers

As many as 77% of people aged 50 and older want to stay in their own home as they age, but only 49% think that they will be able to do so, according to AARP. This is an often-cited number, other data sources report even higher numbers. For example, a

U.S. News and World Report Aging in Place Technology Survey stated:

Although the majority of survey respondents (93%) say aging in place is an important goal for them, 59% feel their home is at least somewhat ready, and only 19% feel that their current home setup is completely prepared for the years ahead. Meanwhile, 41% feel their current setup is minimally ready to not ready at all because their home lacks components such as no-step entry, a voice- or remote-controlled thermostat, virtual assistant devices, and/or height-adjustable products.

Yet, in a FORBES Health online article recently these statistics were Provided:

The Number of Homes Suitable for Aging-in-Place

- A 2020 report by the U.S. Census Bureau estimates only 10% of American homes are "aging ready," meaning they feature a step-free entryway, a bedroom and bathroom on the first floor and at least one bathroom accessibility feature.

- One-third of all poll participants in a 2021 AARP survey said modifications would be necessary in their current residence so they or a loved one could continue to live there should physical limitations occur.

- 79% said bathroom modifications like grab bars or no-step showers would be necessary, 71% noted indoor and outdoor accessibility issues, 61% said they would need an emergency response system and 48% said they would need smart-home devices, such as a voice-activated home assistant or a doorbell camera.

- Aging-in-place home modifications can cost anywhere from $10,000 to $100,000.

This has always been the aging-in-place paradox, most older adults say they overwhelmingly favor aging in place—but very few are doing anything about it. This is the REALTIY of the situation. Further, nearly half of baby boomers have no retirement savings—which equates to limited options for running off to the "right" place (also means half do however).

Summary

So, the aging in place Paradox is real—at least these are the folks I am in contact with. They don't preplan, they do have multiple chronic conditions, they have very limited savings, living in homes that require home modifications they desperately need. How do I know this? Because I hear from them weekly through aginginplace.com.

So often none of this is addressed until the adult children get "the call" that mom fell—and now the crisis-buy of aging in place is set in motion. Few are prepared, few know where to access help, few can afford it. I know this as I said, because I have been answering questions for individuals in this situation from my website for decades now.

Bottom-line is **not everyone can experience aging in the right place**, for those who can I'm delighted for them, and I Hope their ranks grow. But my in-the-trenches experience tells me the inescapable realities. I've had to work where people are, in crisis, needing help like a drowning person needs oxygen.

This is where the challenge lies, working where folks are— not where they theoretically should be. I'm all for that "right" place, but in the meantime so many will be aging in less an optimal place (especially minorities for historical social systems reasons), and that's where most of the help will be required.

In my job you can't just put your head in the sand and throw partisan bombshells. You have to get results.

~Amy Klobuchar, Senior United States Senator from Minnesota

Recently I posted this on a social media site: *Aging in Place can preserve a sense of self as a homeowner and community member, in a time of loss and change that defines aging; known as "Continuity of Self."*

This response came in shortly after posting:

Aging in Place is a misnomer. Aging in the Right Place more accurately represents what you describe.

My follow up:

It isn't a misnomer for many individuals I know...But, yes nothing is 100% (except taxes and death as the saying goes).

Aging in "the Right Place"

There is a movement as of late talking about "aging in the right place" as noted here in a The New York Times:

The expression "aging in the right place" (as opposed to aging in place) is gaining currency among experts who advise older adults. "It's shaped by **personal vision, opportunity and what moves you,** "said Linda P.

Fried, dean of the Mailman School of Public Health at Columbia University.

~Amy Zipkin

The response I got was inspired by reading posts like this one from the Times. And yes, I get it...**In a perfect world aging in the right place would be the standard** and optimal for all. But I don't live in a perfect world and most people I know don't either. Which means most will be aging in place under circumstances less than optimal. In fact, there is a term used for the kind of housing most of us (in the real world) live in called "Peter Pan Housing."

Peter Pan Housing

As mentioned in chapter 1, Jon Pynoos, a professor of gerontology policy and planning at University of Southern California coined the term *Peter Pan homes* for homes that have stairs, inaccessible bathrooms, and inadequate lighting, and they lack many of the safety features that would help people avoid falls. That describes most aging housing stocks we are all growing older in. It's been estimated that 70% of baby boomers will be aging in the suburbs and in rural areas. These are not "the right place" but they are the places where living will occur into old age.

So, "aging in place" is not a misnomer, it's reality. Given this fact, there will be some who will be able to find "the right" place, but most won't. This presents a number of issues for all involved. For gero-entrepreneurs and AIPPs the opportunities are limitless, finding creative ways to bring goods/services to those aging in place.

For adult children the challenges will be daunting at times, juggling work/family/and care giving. For Builders and remodelers, this means new streams of business (aging in place remodeling is the fastest growing segment in the remodeling industry according to the National Home Builders association). And for older adults themselves this will present a mixed blessing; being home has its UPSIDE (comfort of home), but it also has its DOWNSIDE as well (for example isolation).

This is one of the greatest societal challenges facing our nation (it is global as well) and working towards optimal outcomes is the goal, but we can't bury our heads in the sand and label reality a "misnomer."

We must tackle the issues head-on, which means meeting people where are, not where we'd like them to be, but where they are...We need to get results.

Aging in place works until it doesn't.

I'm not entitled to have an opinion unless I can state the arguments against my position better than the people who are in opposition. I think that I am qualified to speak only when I've reached that state.

~ Charlie Munger

I was asked recently to talk with a relative newcomer to environmental gerontology about the aging in place concept. He is a retired professional, in his 80s, and will soon be presenting at a global conference. Before our talk on the phone, I designed a framework concerning two main hot topic issues surrounding aging in place on social media currently. I included some of the thinkers on the side of "aging in the right place" and others on the side of aging in place. This was not intended to be an "us vs. them" framework; again, we are all working towards solutions to a global issue on aging.

Stephen M. Golant, Ph.D.

Golant is a leading national speaker, author, and researcher on the housing, mobility, transportation, and long-term care needs of older adult populations. He is a Fellow of the Gerontological Society of America, a Fulbright Senior Scholar award recipient, and a Professor at the University of Florida. Golant's latest book is Aging in The Right Place,

published by Health Professions Press. Contact him at golant@ufl.eduhttps://boomingencore.co m/en/article/living-places-where-people-are-old-you-good- or-bad-thing

Howard Glickman

Is the author of the book "Caring for Our Parents" and senior fellow at The Urban Institute, where I am affiliated with the Tax Policy Center and the Program on Retirement Policy. I also write a tax and budget policy blog, TaxVox, which you may read at Forbes.com or at http://taxvox.taxpolicycenter.org/ Before joining Urban, I was a senior correspondent in the Washington bureau of Business Weekhttps://www.forbes.com/sites/howard gleckman/2022/03/21/aging-in-place-is-all-the-rage-but-it- is- not-easy/?sh=5a62c66242c3

Some of Their main arguments:

Social Isolation with traditional aging in place "The architecture of Isolation"

-Maintaining home repair costs/remodeling costs only 1-4% of homes have "Visitability" features 1) Non-barrier entrance

2) Bathroom/bedroom on the main 3) 36" doorways

-Lack of qualified caregivers / Costs of in-home help rising

-Lack of transportation with traditional suburban homes (auto-dependent)

-Increasing home values = Increased tax burden

-Burden on family members for care

-Older people will resist Remodeling

-70% OF Boomers live in suburbs or rural areas (Isolating) I can't argue with any of this BTW!

Aging in Place is a Crisis Buy, that is, done under duress most of the time because of a lack of planning ahead.

Arguments for Aging in Place

The Benefits

Aging in place is much more than being in an environment of choice as one gets older, it means home–a place where emotional and functional needs are met. Home is a foundation where family histories are created, and rich memories have been woven from shared experiences. Your home contains a lifetime of cherished objects that support identity and delight the senses. It's also nestled in the community you've cultivated over the years, which is the center of those daily rituals you love so much. You plan to stay; it's where you live.

Emotional Ingredients

"Place attachment" is the preference for home caused by a bond developed through experiences over time. The deeper meaning of home comes from:

- Home as a social center for family and friends to gather
- Home as a source of pride in ownership, social status, and feelings of "rooted-ness" in a community
- Home as a source of independence and stability in the midst of loss and change related to aging ("Continuity of Self")

We really don't need to be given reasons for the emotional ties that fuel our desire for aging in place; but there are some practical reasons to consider.

Practical Ingredients

The home may act as a "health protectant" in a number of ways:

1) The avoidance of nosocomial (Institution-acquired) infections

By living at home (instead of institutional-type housing) exposure to multi-drug-resistant organisms (MDROs) can be minimized.

MDROs have been on the rise for the last several decades due to:

- Poor health care provider hand washing and high staff turn-over
- The era of aggressive antibiotic use creating "super bugs"
- Increased numbers of immune-compromised patients/residents

There is greater control over exposure to pathogens ("bugs") in your own home.

2) The prevention of "Relocation Stress" or "Transfer Trauma"

"Relocation stress" is a set of symptoms and outcomes that result from a transfer of an older adult from a familiar to an unfamiliar environment—the symptoms range from:

- Sleep disturbance
- Cognitive decline / confusion
- Perceived loss of control
- Withdrawal
- Depression
- Failure-to-thrive
- Death

Aging in place may increase the chances of preventing these outcomes by remaining in a familiar environment – wherever you call home.

3) Preserve brain function with "environmental press"

Meeting the challenges of living at home may help support a healthy aging brain with activities such as:

- House cleaning-maintenance and laundry
- Yard work and gardening
- Riding the bus and driving
- Negotiating for goods and services
- Paying bills
- Taking care of pets/ walking them
- Using computers
- Shopping

These activities are all sources of what Professor of Gerontology, M. Powell Lawton called "environmental press" (demands, challenges, and stimulation the environment provides, more in chapter 4). Studies have shown that environmental press/complexity stimulates aging brains to grow new connections and neurons which support learning and memory.

Paradoxically these traditional "burdens" of home ownership may be sources of "environmental press" which support a healthy brain, and in turn aging in place. Institutional living is designed to minimize or eliminate these kinds of daily demands. For some that is the goal, but every form of refuge has its price. Environments with too little challenge or novelty can cause senescence.

Summary

In so many cases it's "Follow the Money" in these arguments (*academics aside). I always ask myself what do the parties have to gain by taking a certain stance on the topic? Most of the time it boils down to two camps: 1) the LTC industry wants you to buy into the Sun City / active senior model or 2) In-home care providers favor aging in place at home. You will notice this play out over and over. That is the free marketplace at work.

In a perfect world, we all could sell our un-age-friendly homes and jet off to the "Right" place where the sun is always shinning, we are all like-minded, no crime, no stress, leisure 24/7, community, green spaces everywhere, all have financial means and high education levels, all needs are inclusively met... But that's not the reality. It's aspirational and worthy of pursuit, but for now, I'm in the trenches like a public health professional meeting people where they are.

All of us who favor aging in place also favor aging in the Right Place; however, most people don't prepare (for a number of systems issues) and will be aging in less-than-optimal environments. Therefore, you must work where people are and with policy changes at local and national levels. That's the least glamorous work, of course.

Having outlined this, I do not wish to frame it as an either/or factional representation of the aging in place. We are all on the same team when it comes to making the world a better place to age in. I hope this helps outline and provide some theoretical scaffolding of some of the issues (as I see them).

CAPS Chat Tip

Aging in Place Doesn't Get Real Until It Gets Personal.

~ Patrick Roden PhD CAPS

Point #3

Aging in Place is about Independence

What Does "Aging in Place" mean? I was asked this question in a recent interview; my answer went something like this:

"**It means enjoying the pleasures of living at home in a familiar environment and community, safely, comfortably, and Inter-Dependently; regardless of age, income, or ability.**" There are some key elements worth un-packing in this definition which I will do here briefly. Let's start with "familiar environment," which encompasses the physical aspects of Home. Our dwellings are really containers of a lifetime of cherished objects that delight our senses and support our identity. This may be easily overlooked, but to the older adult who is experiencing loss and change that defines aging (friends, colleagues, roles, physical abilities, meaning), supporting identity is psychologically adaptive.

Older adults will make adaptive choices in an attempt to maintain existing internal and external structures—and they do this by using strategies tied to their past. In Gerontology, the study of aging, this theory of Continuity of Normal Aging, was posited by Robert C. Atchley, Ph.D., and I've applied the concept to the experience of aging in place.

The Home can be that stabilizing entity in several ways:

1) Self-Identity as a "Homeowner"

2) Member of a community

3) Home filled with meaningful objects support identity and act as psychological anchors; reinforcing who the person was, who they are now, and who they will become

Next, the concept of living "independently" is really a misnomer and a paradox. If you want to be more independent—you're going to have to be more "inter-dependent." Meaning aging in place is a team sport, that is, it happens in the context of support which are often community of one kind or another. This ties into the "safely" notion as well:

1) Informal Network of caregivers (family, friends, church, etc.)
2) Basic Transportation
3) Affordable Housing
4) Increasingly Technology
5) Formal Caregivers

Finally, the aspect of "comfortably" covers both physical and mental for the older adult. Home is the place where we are most deeply ourselves and it's there that we can control access to our most private selves.

The Poet conveys it best:

There is nothing like staying at home for real comfort.

~ Jane Austen

Independence vs. Inter-dependence

Aging-in-place technology theoretically was developed to provide complimentary assistance for older adults seeking "independence." that has always been the selling point—but hear me out, aging in place is NOT about independence. If you have ever helped maintain an older adult in their own home, you know it's done by inter-dependence.

Ok, here's the key take home, aging-in-place technology is about PARENT'S INTER-DEPENDENCE, and YOUR client's fam- ily member's INDEPENDENCE. It may sound counter intuitive but let me unpack this.

Mom and dad boomer have been sold on the idea of "independence," fine you're not going to unearth that one, don't even try. But you know by having the technological capacity to be in frequent contact, monitoring activities, assisting with medical needs, food deliveries, home security, and so much more, that so called "independence" is supported by tech and know-how. This is inter-dependence in its most beautiful and loving form. In many ways aging-in-place technology is seamlessly integrated and non-stigmatizing today—in my day I did not have those options. It was just emerging and clunky, difficult to use, and highly stigmatizing to a generation that had not fully embraced it (high barriers to adoption). So, for me, caregiving and aging in place meant hands-on analog labor intensive. Any little potential fires and I had to get off work, drive several hours, take time away from my responsibilities, and do what I THOUIGHT needed to be done.

The older adults in my family had so called "independence" as historically defined by the aging-in-place industry. However, the collateral damage was my "independence." I would do it all over again, but now there is a more efficient and effective way to supplement care of loved ones.

You now have refined aging-in-place technology easily available from places like BestBuy to set older adults up for aging in place success. Which maintains their Inter-dependence and family member's Independence! READ that again...Analog caregiving is still required, but there is a huge opportunity cost when faced with many of the caregiving scenarios that need attention.

Smart technologies for aging in place can be a key to family independence. When I think back on all the times I invested in false alarms or easy to solve things, to major emergencies, the right technologies could have made the difference between me being on a wild goose chase or having dinner with my wife on a date night (aka peace of mind).

It's not an either/or, informal caregiving is an act of love, most of us will be involved in the process—it's whether you do it smartly with the help of technology, or you don't.

CAPS Chat Tip

Aging in Place "Independence" is Like Sasquatch; I hear A lot About it, I've Just Never Seen it.

~ Patrick Roden PhD CAPS

Summary

Conventional Wisdom Point #1

Never use the term "Aging in Place" when marketing

Author's Take: Use "Aging in Place" don't give into geronto-phobia and views of aging from the last century. Respect where your clients are in life and reward them with non-stigmatizing aging-in-place modifications. Ageism is never good business.

Conventional Wisdom Point #2

Aging in Place vs. Aging in *THE RIGHT* Place

Author's Take: 4% of older adult households have the minimal "visitability" features, they are unprepared, under financed, and have multiple chronic conditions. This is the reality, and you will be working with clients where they are for the most part, often in a crisis. Few will be aging in the right place.

You'll help them with aging in an improved place.

Conventional Wisdom point #3

Aging in Place is about Independence

Author's Take: Aging in place is not about independence, period. The paradox is if your clients want to be more independent, they will have to be more inter-dependent, aging in place is a team sport. Do avoid the term "independence."

*Happy Gerontology is looking at aging only through rose- colored glasses.

What you do matters.

Resources

There are some forward-thinking individuals working to be part of the solution: NUUAGE CoLiving Budget Friendly Shared Housing for Older Adults is a good example.

Atchley RC. A continuity theory of normal aging. Gerontologist. 1989 Apr;29(2):183-90. doi: 10.1093/geront/29.2.183. PMID: 2519525.

3

Aging in Place The Opportunity

Don't concern yourself with the money. Be of service ... build ... work ... dream ... create! Do this and you'll find there is no limit to the prosperity and abundance that will come to you.

~ Earl Nightingale

Decades ago, when I was first learning about aging in place, I heard a very rich businessman give a talk on the source of his success. He used the acronym TNT and went on to describe what each letter stood for. I was sitting on the edge of my seat, it seemed so simple, yet so powerful.

He said, I've become wealthy by asking myself 3 easy questions: Where's the trend? Where's the need? And where's technology headed? He went on to detail how this simple formula made him successful.

I was so taken by this "success formula" I thought could aging in place be a good fit? The concept was mostly academic, not yet in the public's consciousness as it is now. So, I ran it through the model to see.

TNT Model

TRENDS / Demographic Transition, 76 million aging baby boomers, 10, 000 a day turning 65 and will continue to 2030 and beyond. Well, that fits nicely!

NEEDS / 77% to 90% AARP members polled favor Aging in Place over Institutional living. There was not just need, but an overwhelming demand! That fits too!

TECHNOLOGY / GEROTECH is projected to be $36 Billion domestic market, and $82 billion globally by 2030 (Global News Wire). This too was a perfect fit!

Aging in place as an opportunity fit like a glove with the successful businessman's TNT model back then and even more so now! This is great news for aging in place professionals because the mega-trend is only growing with each passing day.

CAPS Chat Tip

In fact, the older I get, the more I believe.

~Mike Davis CAPS Vice President at Oregon Homebuilders Assoc.

The Opportunity by the Numbers

Investors Business Daily recently reported that the Eco- nomic activity People 50 years of age and better is $9.5 TRILLION/year—that's 40% GDP!!! (Might want to read that again).

The Number of Homes Suitable for Aging-in-Place

As reported earlier, a 2020 report by the U.S. Census Bureau estimates only 10% of American homes are "aging ready," meaning they feature a step-free entryway, a bedroom and bath- room on the first floor and at least one bathroom accessibility feature.

One-third of all poll participants in a 2021 AARP survey said modifications would be necessary in their current residence so they or a loved one could continue to live there should physical limitations occur.

79% said bathroom modifications like grab bars or no-step showers would be necessary, 71% noted indoor and outdoor accessibility issues, 61% said they would need an emergency response system and 48% said they would need smart-home devices, such as a voice-activated home assistant or a doorbell camera. Aging-in-place home modifications can cost anywhere from $10,000 to $100,000.

Source: forbes.com/health/healthy-aging/aging-in-place-s tatistics/

Aging in Place is a "Crisis Buy" Opportunity

I was asked recently why I call aging in place a "Crisis Buy?" I first encountered the term at an American Society on Aging Conference several years ago in Chicago. The then acting President and CEO of Home Instead Senior Care was giving a keynote and he mentioned the term—it stuck. Rarely do older adults prepare for aging in place remodeling, in fact, as far back as 2011, a study conducted by the Office of Policy Development and Research's Multidisciplinary Research Team, suggested that most U.S. homes are not fully accessible.

The time to repair the roof is when the sun is shining.

~John F. Kennedy, former U.S. President

Although approximately one-third of units have Level 1 accessibility features (see below) and are potentially modifiable, fewer than 5 percent of units have the features needed to accommodate a person with moderate mobility difficulties. The percentage of wheelchair-accessible units is even smaller; less than 1 percent of all units are equipped with features that would allow a wheelchair user to live independently. The researchers did note that some households might be misreporting features, which could result in underreporting some accessibility elements.

Level 1: Potentially modifiable. Homes in this category have some essential accessibility features but would not be fully accessible without further modifications, including the following:

Step-less entry into the dwelling from the exterior.

A bathroom on the entry Level or the presence of an elevator in the unit.

A bedroom on the entry Level or the presence of an elevator in the unit.

Level 2: Livable for individuals with moderate mobility difficulties. Homes in this category have a minimum level of accessibility that allows a person with moderate mobility difficulties to live in the home. Level 2 homes include all the features of Level 1 homes as well as additional features, including the following: No steps between rooms or rails/grab bars along all steps.

An accessible bathroom with grab bars.

Level 3: Wheelchair accessible. Homes in this category have a minimum level of accessibility sufficient for a wheelchair user to live in the home and prepare his or her own meals. This group includes all the features in levels 1 and 2, and additional features, including the following:

Extra-wide doors or hallways. No steps between rooms.

Door handles instead of doorknobs. Sink handles or levers instead of knobs.

Wheelchair-accessible electrical switches, electrical outlets, and climate controls.

Wheelchair-accessible kitchen countertops, kitchen cabinets, and other kitchen features.

(Accessibility of America's Housing Stock: Analysis of the 2011 American Housing Survey).

Fear of Aging

Much of this lack of planning architecturally for the future is caused by gerontophobia (other causes are noted such as lacking financial means, the knowledge and or, other resources), or the fear of aging. So much so, that aging-in-place re- modeling is considered not as a preventive, but so often as a post-emergency/s "come to Jesus moment" decision. Sadly, a fall can put a quick end to life as it once was for the older adult. Paradoxically, the fear of aging + lack of planning = secondary agers; which actually speeds up the aging process and potentially death...

CAPS Chat Tip

If you want a BIG Opportunity, find a BIG Problem, aging in place is both.

~ Patrick Roden PhD CAPS

A Story of Aging Boomer Trends

I Had a conversation with my sister recently. She is a front-end boomer and I listen to her for trends in that demographic. She has this, let's call it a "caravan" or tribe of women friends of similar age. They have never married, owned and sold businesses, worked hard, saved money, and for the most part did well.

They have a mutual support group (social capital) and during their white wine sessions the talk often turns to life issues confronting them at specific stages. From career, investments, menopause, aging parents, lack of suitable partners, all the big issues.

For example, my sister described her group discussing how once you reached a "certain age" the single men all dried up. The women found this both frustrating and encouraging at the same time. The good part was they found themselves at certain stages in their lives quite capable of doing things that traditionally the men in their lives would be. Fixing gutters, repairing plumbing, painting interiors and dealing with flat tires, all created a self- reliance they didn't anticipate. The group were going to get T-Shirts that read:

"I'M BECOMING THE MAN I ALWAYS WANTED TO MARRY!!

Conversation Shifts

These days, she reports, the conversation topics have shifted. Two predominate themes now at this stage take up much of the discussion. **The first is chronic polypathology** (multiple physical infirmities) due to living life to the fullest physically.

These women were athletic in young adulthood, worked as physical labors in some cases, have been hikers, travelers, skiers, runners, and adventurers—this has an accumulative effect over time (the wear-and-tear theory of aging).

Secondly, being single and not having children, they have had access to disposable income. So, at this stage in life many are "over provisioned," or have too much stuff. Downsizing is a new concern and living with less is important for these women.

The trend is your friend.

~ Martin Zweig

These two Boomer trends provide opportunities for entrepreneurs seeking to solve problems for a segment of the population (more on customer segmenting in chapter 6) that will need help and be willing, and able to pay for it.

Summary

Female Boomer Trend Needs (for a segment of this demo- graphic)

- Chronic PolyPathologies (physical challenges) = Homes requiring modifications
- Over Provisioned (too much stuff) = Downsizing requiring decluttering homes and lives

Aging in Place has an Element of Defiance

MSN posted a piece on aging in place and boomers. It's always eye opening to read the comments. For example, for this post here are a few that stand out:

" Have you ever looked at the cost of a retirement community? **Try 4K a month! I will just stay in my paid for house."**

"What right do we boomers have to live and act as we want to? We're just a burden on society, right? Maybe 'The government' should round us all up and put us in a camp. Everything is our fault."

"My house don't care if you can't afford one or buy one.... I don't care about your housing market, your pretend jobs you think will be needed, or your lack of thought about medical care. It will be the same then as it is now."

"Put a stair chair in for my mom, and it kept her in her house where she wanted to be. Now it's keeping my stepdad in the house where he wants to be. Seniors don't own anybody anything except themselves. To live the best life, they can."

<u>**CAPS Chat Tip**</u>

Read Online Media sources about aging in place then pay special attention to the comments, pure gold!

~ Patrick Roden PhD CAPS

The thread that runs through the comments is defiance. Now, there is always the risk of sample bias, who reads and responds to posts, the source of the content, and other factors, but it's clear the comments suggest boomers are not giving up their homes, feel they have earned the right to do as they please, and a touch of feeling slight hostility towards outside influences.

These themes, although I urge caution in thinking they are representative, do give insights into how some potential cus- tomers for aging-in-place professionals are thinking. How can you employ these insights in your business?

Know the Difference Between Wants and Needs of Your Clients

I had an eye-opening conversation about a book I wrote, with a savvy YouTube book marketing expert. What does this have to do with you and your aging in place business you may ask? Well let me explain, she offered one gem that was hard-hitting:

"**We see potential, but we never know what it will do … but we both felt hesitant to tell you we should market the book as it is right now.**" Ouch, your baby is ugly in other words.

What she alluded to is the difference between WANTS and NEEDS. Seems my book covered NEEDS, but they felt it lacked the allure of WANTS (what she called the "it factor"). What people NEED often isn't what they WANT, and vice versa. I tried not to take it personally and looked for the lesson.

If you are in the business of providing NEEDS (which you are) you better get yourself positioned in WANTS first, or yours will be a path of pain, disappointments, and wasted time. By the way, this has been my lane for decades, trying to get folks interested in aging in place (NEED) before they (WANT) it (I've wised up over the years).

It's always been a challenging sell for several reasons, 1) WWII generation was fiercely independent and didn't fully embrace the idea of needing remodeling for accessibility 2) Boomers were in "not ready for that yet" mode. The good news is the demographics have shifted, and aging boomers are more inclined to embrace remodeling for aging in place, as well as the technology.

Let's unpack this briefly viewing through the filter of a CAPS builder-remodeler, Architect, or universal design consultant— but the principles are widely applicable.

What the Aging-in-Place Professional Knows is Required Needs: ("The Steak")

Finances / Resources Health (functional aging)

Universal Design and Accessible Design Features Aging-in-place remodeling

Aging-in-place Technology

A system in place to achieve "independence" (INTER-dependency)

What the Potential Customer Thinks They Want Wants: ("The Sizzle")

Independence

Preserving one's natural rituals, rhythms, and routines of living at home

Their own aesthetics

Freedom to come and go as they please Control

Sameness Community

Age-Diversity contacts vs. age-segregation Privacy

Control of access to the self from others Safety

Comforts of Home

Preserve memories created over time

Place attachment / Staying Put (not surrendering to convalescence)

The list of NEEDS is often shorter than the list of WANTS. So, the takeaway from my conversation with the savvy book marketer is widely applicable—especially for those of us in the business of aging in place. To avoid the Sisyphean task of trying to convince based on NEEDS, it is better to translate them into WANTS and sell the sizzle, not the steak. An age-old lesson—The key is this: **NEEDS should be a byproduct of Wants,** figure this out and you've built a better mousetrap, and the world will come beating down your door.

Just make sure it's accessible!

CAPS Chat TIP

Person-Centered Aging in Place Design is labor intensive, individualized, and in constant flux.

~ Patrick Roden PhD CAPS

7 Habits Revisited for CAPS

Finally, to get you the aging in place professional in shape for the mega-opportunity you're embarking on, I think revisiting the 7 Habits of Highly Effective People by Stephen Covey is essential. The 7 habits have been adjusted for the aging in place customer market and your business.

Every human has four endowments- self-awareness, conscience, **independent will and creative imagination. These give us the ultimate human freedom... The power to choose, to respond, to change.**

~ Stephen R. Covey

Some of you may remember the 1980-90s organizational su- perstar guru Stephen R. Covey (most of you won't, you're too young!). He went viral before there was such a thing. Covey built a mega-Franchise from his seminal work *The 7 Habits of Highly Effective People.*

Stephen Covey's work on how to create a better human species titled "The 7 Habits of Highly Effective People" was first published in 1989 and has sold over 15 million copies in 38 languages since first its release. It is still referenced to this day as a template on how to succeed in life.

The concepts are timeless and can be broadly applied as I have done here with aging in place. What follows is The 7 Habits of Highly Effective People Aging in Place:

Habit 1: Be Proactive

Aging in Place: Be Proactive; day-in-and-day-out your clients are faced with "choice points" that will have a cumulative effect on their "independence." If they choose what's easy now (not taking the initiative to make aging-in-place remodeling changes, and not doing the things necessary to stay physically/- mentally fit), life will be hard later.

Most people will wait until a crisis ("A Crisis buy") to begin aging-in-place remodeling projects. We know crisis-driven interventions are seldom as effective as proactive ones. Just be ready to deal with families in stress and crisis, being proactive means anticipating this.

Habit 2: Begin with the End in Mind

Aging in Place: Begin with the End in Mind is making the future a part of one's current philosophy. According to the Aging in America study years ago, seniors fear nursing homes over death; so, for most "independence" is a deeply held value and goal.

Think seriously about how much your clients (and you) value the rituals and natural rhythms of simple daily living at home that have been cultivated over the years. Coffee in the morning and read the paper in a favorite chair perched in the front window; after the cat is let out. Or shopping at the grocer where the clerk knows their first name—then have them imagine life without these.

Look around the house and determine what is going to potentially be a challenge for your clients in the coming years. Do an aging-in-place assessment and make a priority list of action items. Is adding a bathroom on the first floor, installing a lift on the stairs, or an access ramp, something we can do now that will keep them in their home 5-10 years from now?

Hosting family over for traditional life events; and being able to have grandkids stay whenever they choose. Does being a grandparent to them mean having a home where grandchildren can find refuge and a place to stay?

Habit 3: Put First Things First

Aging in Place: Prioritizing remodeling goals with budget in mind. What are the "biggest-bang-for-the-buck" aging-in- place remodeling items?

Clients should start by consulting you, the Certified Aging in Place Specialist (CAPS), Architect specializing in Universal design, or Occupational Therapist trained in aging-in-place design.

Together decide using the 80/20 Rule; what 20% of remodeling items, will provide 80% of their aging in place goals. Together decide on priorities and what action items to with.

Habit 4: Think Win-Win or No Deal

Aging in Place: Win-win means considering the concerns of spouses as well as adult children. Staying in one's home may not be the best solution for all parties. Sometimes aging in place is not possible, or desirable. Integrity calls for doing the right thing for the client/s and the ecosystem they are living in, not just making a sale. Sometimes it doesn't make sense, or isn't a safe scenario, doing the right thing may mean walking away from the work.

Habit 5: Seek First to Understand, then to be Understood

Aging in Place: Listen to partners, spouses and extended family/friends, understand their wants or needs for aging-in- place remodeling. Work to gain a complete understanding prior to making any professional recommendations.

Habit 6: Synergize

Aging in Place: Synergize with other family members by sharing aging-in-place goals; ask for feedback and input; form a team-work approach with CAPS professionals; aging in place is a team sport (A good place to exercise this Habit is with the Photo Voice Exercise that will be discussed in chapter 5).

Make the community part of the aging in place team strategy; employ senior services like meals-on-wheels; the local area agency on aging; AARP chapters; churches; See AginginPlace.com for more resources (Inter-dependence).

Habit 7: Sharpen the Saw

Aging in Place: Keep up on new technologies for aging-in- place; visit web sites for developments in universal design; and educate yourself about what's available in the aging in place market. Aging in Place Technology Watch Will Keep you up on the fast-changing home telemetry sector. Keep physically and mentally fit (your body and mind need to be available to you and your clients) for successfully aging in place. Join professional organizations like NAIPC and network with other professionals, attend conferences and continuing education courses. Sign up with LinkedIn and connect with those in the industry.

These 7 habits applied to your aging-in-place business can be a guide to a successful career and the industry as a whole.

CAPS Chat Tip

Think of economic power, and you might just think of boomers. They currently hold a stunning 52.8% of all U.S. wealth. That's not just a big chunk of change — it's half of the country's $156 trillion in assets (fool.com).

Summary

The Number of Homes Suitable for Aging-in-Place

A 2020 report by the U.S. Census Bureau estimates only 10% of American homes are "aging ready," meaning they feature a step-free entryway, a bedroom and bathroom on the first floor and at least one bathroom accessibility feature.

One-third of all poll participants in a 2021 AARP survey said modifications would be necessary in their current residence so they or a loved one could continue to live there should physical limitations occur.

79% said bathroom modifications like grab bars or no-step showers would be necessary, 71% noted indoor and outdoor accessibility issues, 61% said they would need an emergency response system and

48% said they would need smart-home devices, such as a voice-activated home assistant or a doorbell camera.

Aging-in-place home modifications can cost anywhere from $10,000 to $100,000.

According to 2019 data reported by the Census on the Ameri- can House Survey, 51.9% of homes with two or more floors do not have an entry-level bedroom and 38.9% of homes with two or more floors do not have an entry-level bathroom.

(Source: forbes.com, Aging In Place Statistics And Facts In 2024 by Deb Hipp)

The Trend is obvious, the Need undeniable, and the technology for aging-in-place is exploding. The opportunity is clearly laid out in front of you and unlimited for those aging in place pros positioning themselves to ride this wave.

Now get started and make a difference in other's lives, focus on service the money will come.

~ Patrick

What you do matters.

4

Rethinking Aging in Place "Truisms"

The truth is rarely pure and never simple.

- Oscar Wilde, The Importance of Being Earnest

THE BIG 3

1. Smart Technology supports older adults Independence
2. Fix Loneliness by moving into an active assisted living community
3. The burdens of home ownership

1. Smart Home Technology and "Independence"

Aging-in-place technology has great potential to help older adults live inter-dependently, but as you may know, it's not just about gadgets—it's about making those gadgets accessible and practical. The fact that 86% of people over 50 own a cell phone shows they're comfortable with technology in general, still wearables and other devices often end up forgotten or unused, which reduces their effectiveness. It's not just about purchasing the latest technology; it's about integrating it into daily life in ways that are easy to use and truly helpful.

According to [AARP's report "2021 Tech Trends and the 50+](), the pandemic may have been the impetus for more seniors to take the plunge into the world of smart technology. From smartphones and tablets to wearables (like Apple Watch or FitBit), more and more Americans aged 50 and older are buying tech devices. But the biggest jump among this age group has been in the so-called "smart home technology" category.

Between 2019 and 2020, the percentage of seniors who own smart home technology almost doubled, jumping from 10 percent to 19 percent. Additionally, the number of seniors who own a voice- activated home assistant device (like Amazon's Echo where you "wake up" the device by saying, "Alexa...") went from 17 percent in 2019 to 29 percent in 2020.

~ Brad Breeding mylifeset.net

Although there has been an uptick, it remains a relatively low adoption rate of smart home technology among seniors— illustrates that the learning curve for these devices can be a barrier. The complexity of setup and use, combined with concerns about privacy or simply not understanding the technology, can discourage older adults from fully embracing these systems. And the issue of internet access is a significant challenge, as about a quarter of people over 65 are offline. Without the internet, the benefits of connected devices like health monitors or smart home systems simply can't be realized.

To bridge this gap, what is needed are solutions that blend technology with human support: easier setups, clearer instructions, and perhaps some additional tech assistance from family members or service providers. A holistic approach to aging in place means thinking about both the tech and the human side of the equation.

Aging-in-place technology offers many benefits, empowering older adults to live inter-dependently and safely in their homes. Smart home devices such as automated lighting, fall detection systems, and health monitoring wearables enhance safety, monitor health, and simplify daily tasks. These technologies can provide peace of mind for both seniors and their families, offering real-time alerts for emergencies and enabling remote monitoring, which is especially valuable for those with chronic health conditions or mobility limitations.

However, while these technologies offer significant support, relying solely on them can be problematic. Devices can malfunction, be misused, or go unused altogether (as was the case with my aunt) if they're difficult to operate or remember. Internet connectivity issues, high costs, and privacy concerns also limit effectiveness for some seniors. Furthermore, technology lacks the personal, adaptive support that human interactions provide—companionship, emotional support, and hands-on help with issues the devices may not detect.

In our 2024 survey, we found that 47% of seniors report feeling safer while using assistive technologies, compared to 44% of respondents in 2023.

We also found a large increase in respondents who feel more mobile as a result of using assistive technologies like health mobile apps, health trackers, and medical alert devices: 32% in 2024 vs. 20% in 2023.

~ Naru, L., & Beimesche, E. / *Aging in place with assistive tech survey.* U.S. News & World Report

To summarize, aging-in-place technology is a valuable tool, but it should be complementary—not replace human support systems and regular in-person check-ins. Balancing tech solutions with family, friends, and professional caregiving ensures a more holistic approach to aging safely and comfortably at home.

CAPS Chat Tip

Technology alone is not enough.

— *Steve Jobs*

A Summary of some potential problems with aging-in-place technology:

Forgetfulness and Disuse: Many older adults purchase health wearables or safety devices but forget to use them, leading to ineffective technology. Devices may end up unused, such as left on bedside tables or tucked away in drawers.

Complex Setup and Usability: Some smart home devices have complicated setup processes, which may involve numerous steps, failed Wi-Fi connections, and confusing interfaces. This can be frustrating for seniors and deter them from using the technology.

Lack of Familiarity with Tech: While older adults may be familiar with basic technology, navigating advanced gadgets like smart home systems can feel like an obstacle course, leaving many feeling overwhelmed and hesitant to embrace them fully. **Limited Internet Access:** A significant portion of older adults, about 25% of those over 65, lack internet access, preventing them from using connected devices or taking full advantage of digital health and safety features.

Privacy and Security Concerns: Many seniors are wary of sharing personal data through tech devices due to privacy concerns or the fear of security breaches, which can make them hesitant to adopt health monitors, smart home systems, or other connected devices.

Cost of Technology: The financial burden of purchasing and maintaining aging-in-place technologies, especially if devices are not covered by insurance or health programs, can be a barrier for many older adults.

Physical Limitations: Some technologies, such as voice-controlled devices, might not be fully accessible for older adults with hearing or speech impairments, limiting their effectiveness.

Isolation from Support: Seniors who don't have a reliable support system (e.g., family or tech experts) may struggle with troubleshooting tech issues, leading to frustration and abandoning the technology.

Lack of Customization: Many aging-in-place technologies are designed for a broad audience but may not account for the unique needs and preferences of individual seniors, such as cognitive impairments or specific health conditions.

Incompatibility of Devices: Many devices don't work well together, creating a fragmented experience for users who may struggle with different apps, systems, and devices that don't integrate smoothly.

As aging in place CAPS professionals, it is essential to understand the benefits and limitations of smart home technologies for older adults at home.

Here are ten popular aging-in-place smart home technologies that help older adults live inter-dependently:

- **Medical Alert Systems**: Devices that detect falls or other emergencies and automatically contact help. Some have GPS tracking for added safety outside the home.

- **Smart Door Locks**: Keyless entry systems that allow family members or caregivers to access the home easily while ensuring security. Many can be monitored and controlled remotely.

- **Video Doorbells**: These allow seniors to see who is at the door without opening it, providing both convenience and safety. They also often include motion detection and two-way audio.

- **Smart Lighting**: Motion-activated or voice-controlled lighting helps prevent falls by illuminating pathways automatically. Timed lighting can also provide reminders or simulate a normal routine.

- **Health Monitoring Wearables**: Devices like smartwatches that track heart rate, blood pressure, physical activity, and even detect falls, offering valuable health insights.

- **Smart Thermostats**: Programmable thermostats allow seniors to control home temperature easily, even remotely. They can help with energy savings and ensure comfortable living conditions.

- **Medication Dispensers and Reminders**: Automated dispensers provide the right dosage at the right time, with alarms or notifications to ensure medications aren't forgotten.

- **Voice-Activated Assistants**: Devices like Amazon Alexa or Google Assistant can help with daily tasks such as setting reminders, calling contacts, and even controlling other smart devices in the home.

- **Smart Appliances**: Connected appliances like ovens, refrigerators, and washing machines can provide alerts, be controlled remotely, or include safety features to prevent accidents.

- **Home Security Systems**: Systems that monitor the home for intrusions, smoke, or carbon monoxide, with some allowing caregivers to check in remotely, adding an extra layer of protection.

Nobody can bring you peace but yourself.

~ Ralph Waldo Emerson

More on Aging in Place Technology

Who am I to argue with Ralph Waldo Emerson (May 25, 1803 – April 27, 1882), or "Waldo" as his friends used to call him. He was after all, one of the most brilliant thinkers of the mid- nineteenth century. The American essayist, lecturer, philosopher, abolitionist, and poet who led the Transcendentalist movement had much wisdom to share on a litany of topics. However, he's only partially correct about peace being an inside job (note opening quote).

Granted, Waldo didn't have today's technology to think about, but if he did, I feel he might want to refine his line about "NOTHING" bringing peace of mind but yourself. I get his point, but here's mine—aging-in-place technology can also bring your client family members peace. And I'm speaking about your younger client family members (millennials and younger) about technologies designed to help Boomer/Gen X parents with aging in place safely.

Independence vs. Inter-dependence

Aging-in-place technology theoretically was developed to provide complimentary assistance for older adults seeking "independence." that has always been the selling point—but hear me out, aging in place is NOT about independence. If you have ever helped maintain an older adult in their own home, you know it's done by inter-dependence.

Ok, here's the key take home, aging-in-place technology is about YOUR clients' INTER-DEPENDENCE, and the younger family member's INDEPENDENCE. It may sound counter intuitive but let me unpack this.

Mom and dad boomer have been sold on the idea of "independence," fine you're not going to unearth that one, don't even try. But you know by having the technological capacity to be in frequent contact, monitoring activities, assisting with medical needs, food deliveries, home security, and so much more, that so called "independence" is supported by tech and know-how. This is inter-dependence in its most beautiful and loving form. In many ways aging-in-place technology is seamlessly integrated and non-stigmatizing today—in my day I did not have those options. It was just emerging and clunky, difficult to use, and highly stigmatizing to a generation that had not fully embraced it (high barriers to adoption). So, for me, caregiving and aging in place meant hands-on analog labor intensive. Any little potential fires and I had to get off work, drive several hours, take time away from my responsibilities, and do what I

THOUIGHT needed to be done.

The older adults in my family had so called "independence" as historically defined by the aging-in-place industry. However, the collateral damage was my "independence." I would do it all over again, but now there is a more efficient and effective way to supplement care of loved ones.

Your clients now have refined aging-in-place technology easily available from places like BestBuy to set them up for aging in place success. Which maintains their Inter-dependence and younger family member's Independence! READ that again... Analog caregiving is still required, but there is a huge opportunity cost when you are faced with many of the caregiving scenarios that need attention.

Smart technologies for aging in place will be your client's key to Inter-independence. When I think back on all the times I invested in false alarms or easy to solve things, to major emergencies, the right technologies could have made the difference between me being on a wild goose chase or having dinner with my wife on a date night (aka peace of mind).

It's not an either/or, informal caregiving is an act of love, most of us will be involved in the process—it's whether you do it smartly with the help of technology, or you don't.

Summary

Aging in place technology is about their (Boomer/Genx) Inter-dependence and younger family member's Independence.

> *This youthful heart can love you Yes and give you what you need*
> *I said this youthful heart can love you Oh and give you what you need*

But I'm too old to go chasin' you around Wastin' my precious energy
~ Tracy Chapman

Multiple factors are at play with the increased use of aging-in-place-technologies. Often cited reasons are lack of caregivers, costs of in-home care, geographic distance of informal caregivers (aka family) and frankly, the technology is getting better.

Aging-in-place technologies are easily acquired, easily ap- plied, and can make a real difference in keeping older adults safe in the home of their choice. Not to mention peace of mind for family members.

For reviews and what's new in Aging in Place Technology check out: ageinplacetech.com

Aging in Place

The U.S. News and World Report did a recent (2023) Aging in Place Technology survey. The methodology was reported as:

Methodology

Our 360 Reviews team used the third-party survey platform Pollfish to conduct a national survey of 2,000 U.S. adults who are 55- plus. People identifying as female comprised 57% of respondents, while those identifying as male represented the remaining 43%. Responses were then weighted in order to reflect the current U.S. population by achieving equal distribution with known population characteristics.

The article begins, as most do, making the case for the need of aging-in-place technology by providing demographic transition statistics. The U.S. Census Bureau shows those over 55 grew to 55 million in 2020 and will continue to rise. Point taken, the nation is getting older, and technology will play a larger role now and into the future—got it.

Aging in Place Preferred

I found the fact that **93% of respondents favored aging in place** and reported it was an "important goal for them," supports my informal experience when talking with the 55 Plus crowd.

The term "general aging" was given as the main reason adults 55 and overuse health-related technologies. Further, devices they felt made it easiest to age in place included:

- Medical/Health related mobile apps
- Service-related apps (i.e., Instacart)
- Wearables Health/Medical trackers
- Assistive Smart Home Tech
- Medical Alert devices/systems

These are the usual suspects when discussing aging in place technologies.

Reasons

The main reasons given to adopt assistive devices were not surprisingly age-related physical/mental impairments. Also noted were reasons that lowered the barriers to adoption of such technologies:

- Ease of Use
- Ease of Setup
- Accessible via mobile app
- Wireless
- Voice activated
- Discreet design (non-stigmatizing)

Other data was provided, however, the line I found most interesting was this one:

That survey similarly found that 97% of users' children say the medical device system their parents use brings them relief.

This tells me that when marketing aging-in-place technologies to potential end-users, savvy salespeople will remember younger family members in the process and emphasize their "peace of mind (POM)— this could be the factor that makes it all possible.

U.S. News & World Report Aging in Place with Assistive Tech Survey 2023 by Lauren Naru Here: (https://www.usnews.com/3 60-reviews/services/senior-tech-aging-in-place-survey)

The Opportunity

Technology for the aging population is BIG business—how BIG? try $2 Trillion BIG!

So, these are products and services that use artificial intelligence, information technologies, digital advances to improve the quality of life of older adults. And at the conference, the age tech market was estimated to be around $1 trillion, and it's on its way to $2 trillion.

- marketplace.org

Boomers are doing aging differently and pushing back on ageism in every sector of life—including technology.

2. Fix Loneliness by Moving into an Active Assisted Living Community

When the snow falls and the white winds blow, the lone wolf dies but the pack survives.

~ George R.R. Martin, A Game of Thrones

I continue to try to dissuade people and CAPS professionals of the idea that aging in place somehow equates to independence. We in the West have long adopted the rugged individualist motif—the Lone Ranger who is dependent on no one and bravely pulls themselves up from their own bootstraps to Great things. Cultural Success stories are weighted down by this false narrative—THE GREAT MAN theory, is one very hard to purge from our collective psyche in America. This trickles down to damn near every aspect of our lives, including aging in place.

The reality is the lone hero had lots of help along the way that is either overlooked or ignored like a driver speeding through a crosswalk you are entering and doesn't look at you. **To be human is to be interdependent.**

The inability to maintain living at home (aging in place "independence") should not be viewed as a failure somehow. Like you've given up and are now floating downstream in assisted living. This is not a healthy viewpoint and taken on by some entering facilities.

I do worry, however, that individuals think assisted living is somehow going to solve the loneliness problem. I can recall working as an undergraduate in nursing homes and assisted living facilities and seeing individuals who failed to socialize. They would take on a sense of failure being there and give up amid being surrounded by other residents.

They would come down to breakfast, head back to sequester in the isolation of their room—only to repeat the process with lunch and dinner. Over and over for years, assisted living provided no sense of community by their own choosing. Many were once happier at home in so-called "isolation" but living without the sense of surrendering to institutional surroundings and being labeled a "resident."

Of course this is not everyone, many thrive in assisted living (because they need the assistance) after leaving the isolation of aging in place. My point is this, the isolation of aging-in- place so often touted by assisted living advocates is very real, but there is no guarantee they have the solution to it. We know each individual responds differently and requires custom plans for optimal living into old age. For some that's aging in place, for others it's living in long-term care scenarios.

3. The Burdens of Home Ownership

The senior care industry in general, assisted living specifically, will frequently list all the "burdens of home ownership" as reasons to forgo aging in place. They will offer a long and daunting list of items required to upkeep a home, designed to discourage living "independently." This tactic is well intended, and certainly does give the older adult pause.

Some of Their main arguments:

1. Social Isolation with traditional aging in place / 70% boomers living rural or in suburbs

"The architecture of Isolation"

2. Maintaining home repair costs / Remodeling costs

3. Only 5% of homes (accessibility.org) have "Visitability" features 1) non-barrier entrance 2) Bathroom/bedroom on the main 3) 36" doorways PETER PAN housing for those who never grow old!

4. Lack of qualified caregivers / Costs of in-home help rising

5. Lack of transportation with traditional suburban homes (auto dependent)

6. Increasing home values = Increased tax burden

7. Burden on family members for care/ Opportunity costs to business having Female employees gone

You will not get an argument from me on any of their points against aging in place. However, I want you, the CAPS Professional or remodeler, to consider something before you think about throwing in the towel and giving up.

UpSide and DownSide Risks with Aging in Place

I was listening to Dr. Bill Thomas (Eden Alternative) describe the danger of creating "too safe" of an environment where individuals are not allowed the opportunity to take risks that would permit them to grow and thrive. He notes that the term "risk" simply means an outcome that's different than expected. In defining risk this way there are two sides; the familiar downside to risk which is the probability that things are going to turn out worse than expected—and the lesser-known upside to risk where things actually turn out better than anticipated.

Upside of Risk

It is this upside to risk that seems to be lacking in discussions of aging in place and/or Long-Term Care settings, which according to Dr. Thomas are obsessed with the downside—and I agree. This is really a symptom of the "biomedicalization" of aging where the elderly are treated as a disease category to be cared for (paternalistically) by "experts."

One aspect of this paradigm is infantilizing older people and turning them into "patients" or "residents" to be subject to over-protection. The elderly are not seen as capable of human development and growth. The unstated here is that the end of the lifecycle is not worth risking for potential upside benefits. Thomas makes the point that in no other part of the life cycle is risk aversion allowed.

The Upside Risk of Environmental Press (EP)

Aging in place is risky...Older adults are called upon to rise to the occasion daily to meet the demands of *living at home: Drive to the market, mow the lawn, tend the garden, care for pets, and deal with home upkeep/repairs, security, ADLs, laundry, bills, cleaning, cooking, and many other related responsibilities that could, in some cases, be done for them.

These traditional "burdens of home ownership" that many seek to avoid, are really forms of what's called Environmental Press (EP), or forces in the environment that together with individual need evoke a response. And it's in meeting the demands of EP that older adults remain not just physically challenged–but mentally as well. For example, older men lose muscle mass at twice the rate of older women because in retirement women continue to do chores around the house–and "the life of leisure" may not be neuroprotective.

Perhaps it's time we, as a profession, begin to equate aging in place with the upside of risk. As Bill Thomas states: *Lives should include a balance of downside and upside, risks are part of a normal healthy life.*

CAPS Chat

Tip Include Upside Risk.

~ *Patrick Roden PhD CAPS*

---

*It is not always physically, mentally, or economically feasible for many older adults to be aging in place–this does not work for everyone all the time.

Introduction to The Environmental Press Model

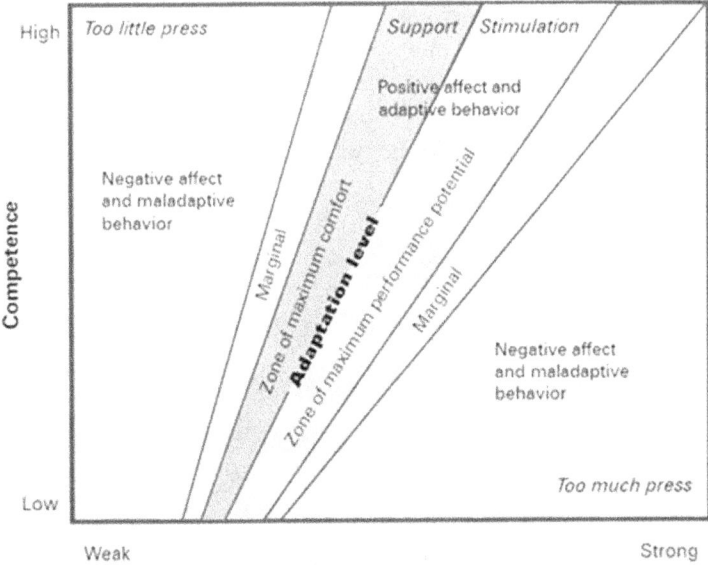

Image Credit: Russell, R. (2016, September 28). *The development of a design and construction process protocol to support occupational therapists in delivering effective home modifications* (Master's thesis).

Environmental Press: Forces in the environment that together with individual need, evoke a response.

The EP model was developed by the country's first environ- mental gerontologist, M. Powell Lawton and is a monumental contribution to aging and the home environment. The EP model is fundamentally depicting **ADAPTATION**; it provides conceptual language about the individual's experience and gives professionals terms to help clients with aging in place.

This model is operationalized as the outcome of the transaction or interaction between the person and the environment. In simpler terms, optimal fit occurs when someone's capacities are consistent with the demands and opportunities within that person's environment. However, if the demands of the environment exceed those of the person and their abilities, there is a person-environment misfit. This model can help key the CAPS professional, Physical / Occupational Therapists or remodeler, in determining the types of environmental changes that must be made to match the individual's abilities.

X-Y Axis

The Y-axis of the graph depicts an individual's competencies that are a result of their functional, biological, sensory/perceptual, cognitive, and social abilities as well as behavioral skills.

The X-axis represents the amount of environmental press or how accommodating their current environment is to their abilities.

Case Study "Jim"

Things to Consider Regarding case study "Jim", a 54-year-old anatomy professor with several chronic conditions, including carpel tunnel. He often takes continuing education courses during the summers. He is living at home.

Below is an example of the process physical or occupational therapist go through in accessing clients at home. For CAPS professionals and remodelers, it is useful to have some under- standing so you can have an idea of the thinking required to better help your clients (my goal for you is to be best in class as a "systems thinking" CAPS professional).

Jim's Y-Axis: Intrinsic Factors and Abilities

Functional: What tasks are currently difficult for Jim to perform?

Biological: Test functioning through ROM and manual muscle testing. What position hurts most / hurts least, etc.

Sensory/perceptual: Sensory deficits in his hands – tempera- ture, light and heavy touch, paresthesia, numbness

Cognitive: There do not appear to be deficits in this area of function.

Social: How has the hand injury affected his social experience? Attending events? Being with friends or students?

Behavioral skills: How is Jim handling his situation? How does he feel about himself? How does he feel others perceive him?

Jim's X-Axis: The Environment

The environment can be made up of 2 conceptualized terms: the physical and the psychosocial.

Physical

His home environment: Investigate his living situation. A 2-story house. What does he do around the house – cook? What utensils does he use? Trouble opening containers? Opening doors? Typing on a computer and replying to emails, writing papers, reviewing notes, transcribing

His environment at school: Opening doors, opening lockers, how does he take notes in class, does he carry around books, required to flip through papers, etc.

His work environment: What position does he sit in to dissect – what is he sitting on / when is he standing / what position is he doing these things in? What tools does he use? Can their handles be built up? Can the positions of the bodies be changed? When does he take breaks? Does he have anything to support his hand during this?

His community environment: How does he get to school – drive? When he goes out for drinks, how does he grip his glass? How does he carry grocery bags?

Psychosocial

Consider the attitudes of those around them: Neighbors, friends, those in positions of authority, other professors, strangers, health professionals, etc.

Compare the tasks Jim performs and how he performs them to the environmental support he currently has. Then ask: What in the environment can be altered to help Jim? What compensation can be made for Jim to help him function better in current living situations? What adaptations can be provided to help him continue to participate in his roles, tasks, and activities?

Summary to this point

The Environmental Press Model is a theoretical framework around which to problem solve as an Aging-in-place professional; to manage and or design the physical environment to fit the needs of the occupant.

The EP is a theoretical framework used to inform practical design intervention strategies for aging in place. Thus, you, the CAPS Professional have practical interventions informed by strong theoretical frameworks.

Choice and control must be congruent with competence.

~ Patrick Roden PhD

The #1 Goal "Goldilocks" Aging in Place (sweet spot-just right)

Provide an environment that is safe yet challenging. Theory looks at 2 things:

1. A person's Personal Competence

<u>Rated LOW to HIGH levels</u>

Deals with the level of personal ability the older adult has and encompasses:

- Their Social
- Their Physical
- Their Psychological
- Intellectual Abilities

2. Environmental Press

<u>Rated WEAK to STRONG</u>

The demands or levels of stimulation and challenges the environment provides

The problem with Institutional and Long-Term Care environments is that they often maintain a level of HOMOGENITY of environmental press—and frequently to the lowest common denominator.

Environmental Press Theory recognizes that individuals have different levels of competencies. To maintain an optimal level of challenge that continues to stimulate the older adult, the environment must be adjusted to EACH INDIVIDUAL level of DYNAMIC competency.

The EP Model assumes that there's an optimal level of adaptation (AL) that needs to exist to nurture the personal competencies of everyone. Too few environmental challenges for the individual with HIGHER levels of personal competencies = Negative/Maladaptive behaviors.

Too few (LOW) individual competencies and existing in an environment with too many challenges = maladaptive behaviors.

The Process Continued

"Titrating" (adjusting) Each individual's dynamic level of competencies to the correct level of environmental stimulation and challenges is labor intensive and ongoing—takes hands on work.

Nutshell: Everyone must be matched to the appropriate type of environmental challenges that will optimize their experience. More complex than just adding rails, roll-in shower, and grab bars; takes a systems approach—sensitizing professionals to understand and be vigilant about "best-fit" environments.

<u>CAPS Chat Tip</u>

Contractors team up with Health Care Professionals like PTs and OTs.

~ Patrick Roden PhD CAPS

Message to CAPS Professionals

Empathetic Lifespan Design is informed by EP theory, and this could be your unfair competitive advantage, the difference between a technician and a professional.

(Avoid Institutional Homogeneity of Environmental Press; untailored and unvarying in its ability to properly sensitize the environment to the varying capacities of the residents in Institutional housing. (Contractors team up with Health Care professionals).

Adaptation Level is a RANGE and shows a continual oscillation around a central point.

Point to Remember: An individual will normally seek his/her own level of Environmental Press.

Highly Competent Individuals will be adapted to COMPLEX environments with HIGH PRESS.

Low Competent Individuals will be adapted to SIMPLER environments with LOW PRESS.

EP can be both:

A) OBJECTIVE (alpha press) Reflecting factors like COMPLEXITY
B) SUBJECTIVE (beta press)

Reflecting the perceived demand character of the environment (When there is a wide divergence between alpha and beta press we speak of delusion)

Independence has at its core the element of choice.
~ Patrick Roden PhD

What You Do Matters. Resources

Christiansen, C. H., & Baum, C. M. (2005). *Occupational therapy: Performance, participation, and well-being.* Slack Incorporated.

M. Powell Lawton (1923-2001) (2001). *Psychology and Aging, 16*(1), 30. https://doi.org/10.1037/h0087879

Russell, R. (2016, September 28). *The development of a design and construction process protocol to support occupational therapists in delivering effective home modifications* (Master's thesis). Retrieved from https://www.researchgate.net/figure/Environmental-Press-Model-Lawton-and-Nehemow-1973_fig2_30 9391395

Tomey, K. M., & Sowers, M. R. (2009). Assessment of physical functioning: A conceptual model encompassing environmental factors and individual compensation strategies. *Physical Therapy, 89*(7), 705–714. https://doi.org/10.2522/ptj.20080213

5

Introducing Choice Architecture and PhotoVoice

Only you can control your future.

~ Dr. Seuss

For a period, I attended meetings in Seattle held by the North- west Universal Design Council Environments for All group. It was at one of the sessions that I met the late Art Mussman, an active senior member of the group.

Art was intelligent, thoughtful, active community volunteer and an advocate of aging in place. He wrote a short post that is a great example of the human need for control and autonomy. Art's advice was to his peers in how to address adult children's fears of remaining home and "independent." I suggest you share these insights with your clients—they will love it.

How To Convince Your Children That You Should Stay In Your Own Home.

The great majority of older people are most comfortable in their own homes. If they feel they can't manage by themselves, then they will consider moving to assisted living or a group home. But their children are always worried about break-ins, falls and heart attacks, and want them to make that move before it is necessary. These are the same children they potty trained and used to worry about when they were late coming home. The shoe is clearly on the other foot now. If you are facing this situation, read on...

Think back to the way that they convinced you to trust them was their making an effort to calm your fears by keeping you informed and acting responsibly. Remember how comforting it was when you realized you could trust them. Now, you must do the same thing!

In order to maintain your independence, you must convince your children through your own behavioral adaptations that you can live independently.

Here's how:

1. **Eat. Don't skip meals.** If you aren't hungry, don't eat much. Keep your refrigerator and pantry well stocked with the food you eat. Get rid of the spoiled, moldy, and stale stuff. Occasionally, invite your children over for a meal. Be a good hostess, use the good dishes, stay relaxed and within yourself.

2. **Organize your finances and pay your bills.** Your children will worry that you will be cheated. Budget. Give your charity money to your own church or a charity that you are familiar with. Suppress the urge to give money to anyone with a sad story, especially those on TV. Don't give any money to people who phone you or come to your door unasked, and that includes repairmen. Ask your children for help with selecting repair people and organizing major financial operations.

3. **Keep your home clean and uncluttered.** One of the clearest signs of dementia is living in clutter: old newspapers, cans, bottles, mail, and other junk. Get rid of furniture and other household items you no longer need. A lot of it will still have good use left or sentimental value, and it is an act of charity to recycle this stuff. If it is too much for you to dust, vacuum, wash windows, mow the lawn and weed the flowerbeds, hire help to do it. If you can't afford that, turn to your faith community or local Senior Assistance for help in finding free chore services.

4. **Take care of your physical self.** See your doctor and dentist regularly. Take your medications, brush your teeth, and exercise every day. Bathe often and wear clean clothes. If you have a chronic illness, such as diabetes, have a good treatment plan and stay with it. Go to a fall prevention class. Watch your weight, blood pressure, and cholesterol.

5. **Stay in the mainstream.** Neighbors, friends, clubs, children, grandchildren, church groups and the like cannot only fill your life

with purpose, but can also support you when you need help, cheer you up when you are ill, and walk with you in daily living.

6. **Use community services.** The government and many private organizations provide services to assist you. For example, there is a bus service that will come to your door at a specified time, take you where you want to go, and bring you home when you are finished. There are organizations that will bring prepared meals to your home. You can get help with your rent or utility bills if you cannot pay them. The good news is that you don't have to hunt for these services. Just call your local Senior Services and tell them what you need.

~ Art Mussman

CAPS Chat TIP

At the heart of aging in place is the notion of control.

~ Patrick Roden PhD CAPS

Another Northwest Universal Design Council Environments for All group member I met during that time was Emory Baldwin AIA. He sent this thought-provoking piece his father shared with him; after contemplating the merits of institutional living. This will get you thinking about how society treats its "interned" and I mention is here to make a point about human autonomy.

Subject: Jail vs. Nursing Home

Let's put the seniors in jail and the criminals in a nursing home. This way the seniors would have access to showers, hobbies,

and walks, they'd receive unlimited free prescriptions, dental and medical treatment, wheelchairs etc. and they'd receive money instead of paying it out.

They would have constant video monitoring, so they could be helped instantly, if they fell, or needed assistance. Bedding would be washed twice a week, and all clothing would be ironed and returned to them.

A guard would check on them every 20 minutes and bring their meals and snacks to their cell. They would have family visits in a suite built for that purpose. They would have access to a library, weight room, spiritual counseling, pool, and education.

Simple clothing, shoes, slippers, P.J.'s and legal aid would be free, on request. Private, secure rooms for all, with an exercise outdoor yard, with gardens. Each senior could have a P.C. a T.V. radio, and daily phone calls. There would be a board of directors, to hear complaints, and the guards would have a code of conduct, that would be strictly adhered to.

The "criminals" would get cold food, be left all alone, and unsupervised; lights off at 8pm, and showers once a week. Live in a tiny room and pay $5000.00 per month and have no hope of ever getting out.

Justice for all...

Mr. Baldwin's piece is of course tongue in cheek; however, it does make a point. What is left out of the argument is the strong human need for autonomy and control. One of my favorite lines of all time is from the Eagles song *Lying Eyes* "Every form of refuge has its price," and both venues lack personal agency (autonomy and control). So, for many, neither jail nor nursing home are a desirable option.

The need for control and autonomy are fundamental and Art Mussman had provided a roadmap that was very popular among his peers because he tapped into a marketing concept known as Autonomy Bias.

Autonomy Bias

Humans have an innate desire to be in control of themselves and their surroundings. Marketers who can give their customers some sense of control, including the opportunity to co-create or to make choices, will appeal to those customers. However, providing too much choice, or providing choices that are not easily distinguishable from one another, can put off customers and produce a negative effect on response.

~ Nancy Harhut, Using Behavioral Science in Marketing From the website verywellmind.com autonomy is described

as involving making independent decisions that align with personal values and goals instead of being coerced by external forces. In psychology, autonomy is viewed as a fundamental human need. It is essential to individual well-being, motivation, and psychological health (see "Photovoice" for aging in place below).

We humans have an almost overwhelming need to exert some level of control and autonomy over ourselves and our environments. This is "Autonomy Bias" is one of the most powerful drivers in human behavior (and a key to your business success). Further, studies have shown that control and autonomy might even be a biological necessity.

For example, researchers Ellen Langer and Judith Rodin conducted a field experiment in 1976 to investigate the effects of choice and enhanced personal responsibility on the well- being of elderly individuals in a nursing home. The study (18 months long) involved two groups: an experimental group given more control over their daily activities and living environment (movie choices, furniture arrangement, watering and caring for a plant in the room) and a control group with less autonomy (those choices were made for them). Results showed that the experimental group experienced significant improvements in alertness, active participation, and overall well-being compared to the control group. These findings highlight the importance of personal agency and decision-making in promoting the mental and physical health of elderly individuals in institutional settings.

How significant? Well, here are the numbers:

1. **Alertness and Activity Levels:**

- The experimental group showed a 93% increase in alertness and active participation compared to only a 21% increase in the control group.

2. **Happiness and Well-being:**

- 48% of the experimental group reported feeling happier and more vigorous, compared to 25% in the control group.

3. **Nursing Staff Ratings:**

- Nursing staff reported that 71% of the experimental group had improved in overall functioning, while only 30% of the control group showed improvement.

4. **Health and Mortality:**

- After 18 months, the mortality rate was significantly lower in the experimental group (15%) compared to the control group (30%).

These statistics underscore the positive effects of increased personal responsibility, choice and autonomy on the mental and physical health of elderly individuals in institutional settings.

The important point for you the AIPP to get is the role of choice as being essential to human flourishing. From Dan Russell's 2020 Vivid Labs article. "Autonomy Bias," "The existence of a choice means a person has autonomy, and the existence of autonomy gives a person confidence that they are in control." When people have choices, they feel in control. And feeling a sense of control answers the deep-seated human need for autonomy (Nancy Harhut, Using Behavioral Science in Marketing).

Bottom line, when individuals take some action, it gives them a sense of control over their circumstances. This seems obvious on the surface, but the implications for you the AIPP and your business are huge.

Further, to increase your success at marketing aging-in-place remodeling services, Harhut has a tip she read from author Roger Dooley's *Neuromarketing* blog. Dooley describes "four words that double persuasion," BYAF which stands for "but you are free." This simple phrase, according to research done by Christopher Carpenter of Western Illinois University reviewed 42 studies involving 22,000 participants and found the BYAF technique can double your success rate (found in Using Behavioral Science in Marketing).

That is a remarkable finding and could easily be integrated into your marketing strategy for a competitive advantage.

Again, I am not in support of manipulating people into buying services they don't want or need. Having noted this, I believe strongly in what the AIPP does and how your business can make individual lives better living at home. Maintain integrity in your dealing with clients and always be upfront and honest.

Having emphasized this, there are forms of messaging that can trigger autonomy bias, and if done in the spirit of service, can with integrity, make a convert of a potential client on the fence.

Expert marketer Nancy Harhut offers one such line she encountered: "You're facing an important decision and if you don't act quickly someone else will decide for you." That is a thought-provoking statement, but relevant for the kind of services you will be offering clients.

Personally, I would soften the language to not come across too pushy yet keep the sentiment of the line intact. "I understand you're facing an important decision; I like to tell my clients that if they fail to act soon, in the future someone else might be deciding for you."

The objective is to get the client thinking about hiring your services all the while maintaining a sense of control by subtly triggering autonomy bias.

CAPS Chat Tip

Look for ways to Provide Choice and Control into your Pitch to Potential Clients.

~ Patrick Roden PhD CAPS

Marketing expert Nancy Harhut makes the point that Providing only one option to the customer is a mistake. She suggests, "When possible, offer two or three. This will prompt people to choose between them, instead of focusing on whether or not they want to respond at all." Harhut makes the assertion that "Marketers looking to trigger autonomy bias can certainly do so by offering their customers and prospects a choice."

The fascinating hidden gem in presenting the client a choice lies in a phenomenon known as "Hobson's Choice." As Harhut describes it, when presented with only one option the potential client will focus on whether or not they want the individual option. But, when two or three options are presented the decision shifts from "do I or do I not want this? to "Which of these options would I like?

Here is an example of 3 levels of service that could be offered by you the Certified Aging in Place Specialists (CAPS) focused on progressively enhancing home safety and accessibility:

1. **Essential Safety Modifications (Level 1)**
   This level focuses on making basic, cost-effective changes to enhance immediate safety and accessibility.
   - **Grab Bars and Handrails**: Installation in bathrooms, stairways, and other critical areas.
   - **Improved Lighting**: Adding brighter lights, especially in hallways, staircases, and entryways to reduce fall risk.
   - **Non-Slip Surfaces**: Applying non-slip treatments to floors, particularly in bathrooms and kitchens.

2. **Enhanced Mobility Support (Level 2)**
   Level 2 involves modifications that improve mobility and ease of movement within the home.
   - **Threshold Ramps**: Installing small ramps at doorways to eliminate tripping hazards and ease wheelchair access.
   - **Wide Doorways**: Widening doorways to accommodate walkers and wheelchairs.
   - **Accessible Entryways**: Creating a zero-step entry with a ramp or lift to the main entrance of the home.

3. **Comprehensive Comfort Enhancements (Level 3)**
   Level 3 includes more extensive modifications to ensure overall comfort and usability of the home.
   - **Bathroom Modifications**: Installing walk-in showers or tubs, adjustable showerheads, and comfort-height toilets.
   - **Kitchen Adjustments**: Lowering countertops, installing pull-out shelves, and ensuring all frequently used items are within easy reach.
   - **Smart Home Features**: Implementing simple smart home devices such as voice-activated lights, thermostats, and security systems to enhance convenience and safety.

These basic tiers provide a structured approach to gradually increasing the safety, accessibility, and comfort of a home for aging in place, starting with essential modifications and progressing to more comprehensive solutions. You, the AIPP can adjust services according to individual client requirements— but the idea is to offer a few levels of services to provide clients with choices.

The take home message is this; by employing autonomy bias messaging in your marketing proposal control is placed into the hands of your clients.

Choice architecture

A final word of caution when presenting potential clients with choices. The term "choice architecture" was created by Richard Thaler and Cass Sunstein in their 2008 book *Nudge: Improving Decisions about Health, Wealth, and Happiness (Thaler, Richard; Sunstein, Cass (2008). Nudge: improving decisions about health, wealth, and happiness. Yale University Press. ISBN 978-0-300- 12223-7)*.

Choice architecture is about designing how choices are shown to people and how that influences their decisions. Here are three examples:

1. **The Number of Choices Presented**:
- Having too many options can overwhelm people, making it hard to decide.

- Example: A restaurant with only a few menu items helps customers choose more easily than one with hundreds of options.

- Behavioral economists have shown that in some instances presenting consumers with many choices can lead to reduced motivation to make a choice and decreased satisfaction with choices once they are made. This phenomenon is often referred to as choice overload, Overchoice or the tyranny of choice (Wikipedia).

2. **The Manner in Which Attributes are Described**:
- How information is presented affects choices. Choice architecture refers to the deliberate crafting of decision-

making environments. By subtly shaping how options are presented, choice architecture influences individual decision-making, often without their explicit awareness (thedecisionlab.com).

- Example: Saying a yogurt is "90% fat-free" sounds better than "contains 10% fat," even though both mean the same thing.

- Be aware of how you frame your services; it will impact the client's decisions. "Aging-in-place home modifications can cost anywhere from $10,000 to $100,000." Vs. "In 2024, the projected national average cost of assisted living is $5,665 per month; however, depending on the specific location and community, monthly costs might be significantly higher" (source: homecaremagazine.com / theseniorlist.com). This deliberate crafting of the costs of aging-in-place modifications is presented instead as costs of assisted living.

3. **The Presence of a Default**:
    - Setting a default option that happens if no choice is made can guide decisions.

    - Example: Automatically enrolling employees in a retirement plan unless they opt-out encourages saving.

For the CAPS Professional offering Levels as a package helps clients make a simple choice of level 1, 2, or 3, which includes multiple aging-in-place features by default.

4. **Essential Safety Modifications (Level 1)**
    - **Grab Bars and Handrails**: Installation in bathrooms, stairways, and other critical areas.

    - **Improved Lighting**: Adding brighter lights, especially in hallways, staircases, and entryways to reduce fall risk.

    - **Non-Slip Surfaces**: Applying non-slip treatments to floors, particularly in bathrooms and kitchens.

The bottom-line is don't overload the client with choices, build in path-of-least-resistance options which sound more appealing to your clients and allow for easy decision making.

Introduction to PhotoVoice

Photovoice is a process (research tool) by which people can identify, represent, and enhance their community through a specific photographic technique. It entrusts cameras to the hands of people to enable

them to act as recorders, and potential catalysts for social action and change, in their own communities. It uses the immediacy of the visual image and accompanying stories to furnish evidence and to promote an effective, participatory means of sharing expertise in creating healthful public policy.

The 3 goals of the photovoice method

Goal 1: To enable people to record and reflect their community's strengths and concerns

Goal 2: To promote critical dialogue and knowledge about personal and community issues through large and small group discussions of photographs

Goal 3: To reach policy makers

From the point of view of the photographers the key function of Photovoice is to give voice to individuals who are the least powerful in society. Often this is due to poverty, race, class, gender, and for our purposes here, older.

Armed with cameras, these individuals can capture aspects of their environment and experiences not accessible to others. The photos, often with captions, are then used to show their lives to the public and policy makers in power. This is done with the intent to help spur change.

Empowering Through Participation Also known as "participatory photography," Photovoice is often used by marginalized groups to provide insights into how they view their circum- stances and their prospects for the future.

The actions taken with the photovoice process; taking pho- to graphs and telling stories as they relate to the photographs, are thought to be empowering. And with the feeling of empowerment, community members are likely to possess greater authority to advocate for an improved quality of life for themselves and the members of their communities.

Photovoice was developed by Caroline C. Wang and Mary Ann Burris in the 1990s.

PhotoVoice Applied to Aging in Place

Here's how PhotoVoice can be applied to aging in place:

1. **Capturing Everyday Life**: Participants, typically older adults, are provided with iPhone cameras and encouraged to document their daily lives, routines, and surroundings. These photographs serve as visual narratives, offering researchers and policymakers a firsthand glimpse into the lived experiences of aging individuals.

2. **Identifying Challenges and Assets**: Through the pho- to graphs taken, participants can highlight both the challenges they encounter in aging in place, such as mobility issues, social isolation, or inadequate housing, as well as the resources and strengths within their communities that support their ability to remain independent.

3. **Facilitating Dialogue**: The photographs act as catalysts for group discussions where participants can reflect on the meanings behind their images, share personal stories, and articulate their needs and preferences related to aging in place. These discussions foster a sense of community and solidarity among participants while also providing researchers with rich qualitative data.

4. **Informing Policy and Design**: The insights gained from PhotoVoice projects can inform the development of age- friendly policies, programs, and urban designs that better support the needs and preferences of older adults. By directly involving older adults in the research process, policymakers and designers can ensure that their initiatives are grounded in the lived experiences and voices of those they seek to serve.

5. **Promoting Advocacy and Empowerment**: Participating in PhotoVoice projects empowers older adults to advocate for change

by sharing their stories and perspectives with a wider audience. Through exhibitions, presentations, or publications, participants can raise awareness about the challenges and strengths of aging in place, advocate for policy reforms, and challenge ageist stereotypes.

Step-by-Step Guide for Using Photovoice in CAPS Remodeling

1. **Preparation**:
- **Introduction to Photovoice**: The CAPS professional ex- plains the concept of Photovoice to the homeowner and the adult child, emphasizing its purpose and process.

- **Instructions on Photography**: Provide basic instructions on how to use their iPhones to take clear and relevant photos, focusing on areas that might present safety or accessibility issues.

1. **Individual Photo Sessions:**

- **Homeowner's Session**: The homeowner uses their iPhone to take pictures of areas in their home and surroundings that they perceive as problematic or challenging. These could include stairs, bathrooms, kitchen areas, lighting, entrances, etc.

- **Adult Child's Session**: The adult child separately takes their own set of photos, focusing on the same or different areas based on their perspective of what might pose difficulties for the homeowner.

- **CAPS Professional's Session**: The CAPS professional con- ducts their own assessment and takes photos, leveraging their expertise to identify potential issues that may not be immediately obvious to the homeowner or the adult child.

2. **Photo Review Session:**

- **Gathering and Organizing Photos**: Collect all the photos taken by the homeowner, the adult child, and the CAPS professional. Organize them into categories (e.g., entryways, bathrooms, hallways).

- **Group Discussion**: Arrange a meeting with all three parties present. Display the photos in a comfortable setting where everyone can see them (e.g., on a large screen or printed out).

3. **Identifying Areas of Agreement and Concern:**

- **Sharing Perspectives**: Each person explains the rationale behind their photos, discussing why they chose to highlight specific areas.

- **Finding Common Ground**: Identify areas where all three parties agree on the need for attention. These are likely to be high-priority areas for remodeling or modification.

- **Highlighting Differences**: Discuss areas where there are differing opinions. The CAPS professional can provide expert input to mediate and explain why certain areas might need attention even if not initially recognized by the homeowner or adult child.

4. **Developing a Plan:**

- **Prioritizing Issues**: Create a list of prioritized issues based on the discussion. Focus on addressing the most critical safety and accessibility concerns first.

- **Planning Modifications**: The CAPS professional can outline potential modifications or improvements for each identified area, incorporating feedback from both the homeowner and the adult child.

- **Next Steps**: Develop a timeline and plan for implementing the necessary changes, including budgeting, sourcing materials, and scheduling work.

Example Outcomes

- **Common Agreement**: All parties might agree that the bathroom is a high-risk area needing grab bars and non-slip flooring.

- **Differing Views**: The adult child might highlight a need for better lighting in the hallway, which the homeowner initially did not see as an issue.

- **Expert Insight**: The CAPS professional might identify a need for wider doorways to accommodate potential future use of mobility aids, a consideration not previously recognized by the homeowner or adult child.

Benefits of Using Photovoice in CAPS Remodeling

- **Enhanced Communication**: Provides a visual and concrete way for all parties to communicate their concerns and ideas.
- **Empowerment**: Empowers the homeowner to actively participate in the remodeling process, ensuring their needs and preferences are considered.
- **Comprehensive Assessment**: Ensures a thorough assessment by incorporating multiple perspectives, leading to more effective and tailored solutions.

By using Photovoice, the CAPS professional can facilitate a collaborative and inclusive approach to home remodeling, ensuring the home environment is safe, accessible, and comfortable for the aging homeowner.

Employing the Photovoice techniques with your aging-in- place clients tap into 3 key marketing principles:

The Law of Social Proof

Agreements with family members, friends, and you the AIPP, can motivate the homeowner because human nature is to con- sider others' opinions when in new situations.

The Law of Story Telling

The Photovoice process will stimulate story telling by all parties, which builds trust—and people buy from those they trust.

Autonomy Bias

People have a strong desire (even a biological imperative) to be in control of themselves and their environments. The Photovoice technique involves the homeowner in the process and decision making providing a sense of ownership and control in the outcomes.

Overall, PhotoVoice offers a powerful tool for collaboratively exploring the complexities of aging in place and working towards creating more inclusive and supportive environments for older adults.

What You Do Matters.

Resources

Harhut, N. (2022). Using behavioral science in marketing: Drive customer action and loyalty by prompting instinctive responses. Kogan Page.

Langer, E. J., & Rodin, J. (1976). The effects of choice and enhanced personal responsibility for the aged: A field experiment in an institutional setting. Journal of Personality and Social Psychology, 34(2)

PhotoVoice [PhotoVoice | Ethical photography for social change](#)

Thaler, R. H., & Sunstein, C. R. (2008). Nudge: Improving decisions about health, wealth, and happiness. Yale University Press.

6

Planning Fallacy and the Consumer Decision Model

If you can't be a good example, then you'll just have to be a horrible warning.

- Catherine Aird

The Planning Fallacy refers to the tendency to underestimate task-completion times.

The planning fallacy is a cognitive bias that refers to the tendency for individuals to underestimate the time, costs, and risks involved in completing a future task or project, especially when they are personally involved in the planning process. This bias leads people to make overly optimistic predictions about how long it will take to complete a task or achieve a goal, often resulting in delays, budget overruns, and unmet expectations.

Lovallo and Kahneman (2003) expanded the original definition of the Planning Fallacy to the underestimation of the time, costs, and risks of future actions and at the same time overestimate the benefits of the same actions resulting in time overruns, budget overruns and benefit shortfalls.

An excellent example is The Sydney Opera House which Started 1 March 1959, expected completion date was 1963. A scaled-down version opened in 1973 a decade later The original cost was estimated at $7 million, the final costs after delays ended up being a whopping $102 million (http://en.wikipedia.org/wiki/ Planningfallacy).

Interestingly, this bias seems to affect predictions about one's own task completion—yet has been shown that when we observe others and are asked to predict their completion times, we have a pessimistic bias and OVERESTIMATE the time it will take someone else to complete a given task.

Conclusion

We just aren't good at being realistic; we envision everything going exactly as planned; no unexpected illnesses, hard-drive crashes, or other Murphy's Law happenings.

Key features of the planning fallacy

1) **Underestimation of Time:** People tend to underestimate the amount of time required to complete a task or project, focusing on the best-case scenario and neglecting potential delays or obstacles.

2) **Overconfidence:** Individuals may overestimate their abilities or resources, leading them to believe that they can accomplish a task more quickly or efficiently than is realis‐ tic.

3) **Neglect of Past Experience:** Despite past experiences of similar tasks taking longer than anticipated, individuals often fail to adjust their estimates accordingly, assuming that this time will be different.

4) **Optimistic Bias:** There is a tendency for people to focus on positive outcomes and ignore or downplay potential risks or uncertainties, leading to overly optimistic predictions.

The planning fallacy shows up everywhere—from big construction projects to business plans and even our personal goals. It's that classic optimism trap: we think things will go faster and smoother than they do. Decision-makers need to know about this bias to avoid underestimating timelines and blowing through budgets. Beating the planning fallacy takes a few tricks: ask for a reality check from others, dig into past experiences, factor in the messy, unpredictable stuff, and always add a little buffer time for those "surprise" setbacks (because they're almost a guarantee!).

CAPS Chat Tip "AKRASIA"

The state of acting against one's better judgment.

Example = Procrastination

Seniors Who Put Off Remodeling Projects Risk Injury

Larry Hume had spent 35 years in the general remodeling and construction business when his mother and father-in-law each fell ill. The aftermath of their recovery didn't just take a toll on them, it changed the direction of Hume's professional life.

"My mother and father-in-law both got ill, and both went into wheelchairs," said Hume, owner of Accessible Home Remodeling in Tucson, Ariz. "There was no access throughout their house. Getting in the front door and getting in the bathroom (were the) two biggest problems."

Hume earned his Certified Aging in Place Specialist (CAPS) accreditation. Now, instead of general remodeling, he focuses on helping people who are aging or in poor health, or those with special needs to stay safely in their homes by making their homes more accessible. The market is huge: about 76 million baby boomers are approaching or at retirement age, and many of them are having issues Hume saw firsthand in his own family.

CAPS remodelers are trained in the technical and service skills "in the fastest growing segment of the residential remodeling industry: home modifications for the aging-in-place," according to the National Association of Home Builders. CAPS professionals evaluate a client's medical condition, look for potential fall hazards or obstructions in the home, and recommend solutions to make the home safer.

Several national studies show that falls are the leading cause of death from injuries for elderly people. More than half of those falls occur in the home.

Studies suggest that a third of those accidents could be prevented through home- modification designs.

"My mother was a prime example," Hume said. "She fell in her bathroom, hurt her ankle and busted her head open." Hume says his personal situation is played out in virtually every aging-in-place project he's been involved with, and he strongly recommends that anyone facing an accessibility issue take action before the remodeling is absolutely necessary.

"In 2009, I installed 98 grab bars, and 96 of them were after (the customer) had already fallen," Hume said. "The biggest thing is to be proactive. I would say all my clients should have done it 10 years ago, so they could enjoy it. Baby boomers are too proud to (ask for) a grab bar. They (would rather) step over the bathtub, squeeze through the door or step over a curb going in the house."

CAPS Chat Tip

Falls Steal Dreams.

~ Louis Tenenbaum "Mr. Aging-in-Place"

The Stages of Change / SCM

Having established the challenge of resistance to aging-in- place remolding services I would like to introduce The Stages of Change Model (SCM). It is relevant because as CAPS professionals we are asking our clients to make changes. For many, change is first equated with loss—human nature is such that we fear loss over gains. Understanding the Stages of Change our clients may be going through can be an asset for you and ultimately your bottom line.

Here is the SCM as applied to aging in place (the LinkedIn article in part).

Greek philosopher Heraclitus noted: "You never step in the same river twice." In other words, change is constant. Flux is the natural order of things and requires continual adaptation or there will be consequences.

For example, take the battle of Jena which was lost 20 years AFTER the death of the Prussian king Frederick—nonetheless, he was blamed. The defeat was attributed to the Prussian army's short-sighted reliance on perpetuating Fredrick's historically successful tactics.

Instead, what the defeated Prussian army should have done (in hindsight) was adapt to the changes in the art of war. Had they made appropriate adjustments the outcome may not have been victory for Napoleon.

Aging in many ways is like that river in a continual state of change, and like a nimble army it takes us by surprise:

Old age is the most unexpected of all the things that happen to a man.

–Leon Trotsky (Lev Davidovich Bronstein), Diary in Exile, 1935

To cope successfully with the unexpected, there must be adaptation to the stages of change associated with aging. I was recently reminded of the stages of change when a psychology professor came into the clinic where I was working for treatment. He was carrying under his arm a book by James Prochaska. We began to discuss Prochaska and Carlo DiClemente's useful theory called the Stages of Change Model (SCM).

The SCM was developed by looking at how smokers were able to give up their habits. The model can be applied to a broad range of behaviors including weight loss, injury prevention, and even making home modifications as we age. The basic idea is that changes in behavior don't happen in one step. Instead, people seem to progress through stages on the way to successful change. And each individual progresses at their own rate through the stages.

The stages of change:

- Precontemplation (Not yet acknowledging that there is a problem behavior that needs to be changed)
- Contemplation (Acknowledging that there is a problem but not yet ready or sure of wanting to make a change)
- Preparation/Determination (Getting ready to change)
- Action/Willpower (Changing behavior)
- Maintenance (Maintaining the behavior change) and
- Relapse (Returning to older behaviors and abandoning the new changes)

Applied to Aging In Place

For the AIPP, knowing the stages can provide context to where the client/s is in terms of making change. For example, say one spouse sees the need for home modification and the other doesn't—telling someone who is in the "pre-contemplation stage" that they must go along with the changes may not work. The individual is not ready to make the changes yet.

Everyone must decide for themselves when a stage is completed and when it is time to move on to the next stage:

Stage One: Precontemplation

In the precontemplation stage, individuals do not think seriously about changing and aren't interested in help. People in this stage defend their current bad habits and do not feel it is a problem. They may be defensive in the face of other people's suggestions to make change.

"We don't need grab bars in the bathroom, that's for old people."

Stage Two: Contemplation

In the contemplation stage individuals have an increasing awareness of the personal consequences of their bad habits and they spend time contemplating their problem. Although they are capable of considering the possibility of changing, they're ambivalent about it and weighing the pros and cons.

"Tom fell the other day in his bathroom and broke a hip. Now he can't meet us for tennis next week...I wonder if a grab bar would have prevented his fall?"

Stage Three: Preparation/Determination

In the preparation/determination stage, individuals have made the commitment to make a change. Motivation for changing is reflected by statements such as:

"I've got to do something about this — this is serious. Something **must change.** *What can I do? I talked with Tom, and he has now installed*

grab bars and other universal design elements into the house...I'm going to visit maybe this is something we should do too."

Here they make small steps toward change.

Stage Four: Action/Willpower

This is the stage where individuals believe they have the ability to change their behavior (internal locus of control) and are actively involved in taking steps to change their bad behavior by using a variety of techniques.

"I'm impressed with Tom's aging-in-place home modifications. They were beautiful and have increased the safety and resale value of his home. I've called a Certified Aging In Place Specialists to come over next week for an assessment."

Stage Five: Maintenance

Maintenance involves the ability to avoid any temptations to return to the bad habit. The goal of the maintenance stage is to maintain the new status quo. People in this stage remind themselves of how much progress they have made towards change.

"This is great, we've made home modifications, and it is a big improvement. I'm going to read up on aging in place and see if we could make more changes. This really was the right thing to do; I don't know why we waited. We've really made progress towards our goal of independent living."

Relapse

The path to successful change for most people involves the experience relapse.

Individuals here can be discouraged and feel a sense of failure. *"Tom, I tripped over the newspapers piled up on the stairs and I'm calling you from my hospital bed. I wasn't going to let that happen and now I'm not feeling so independent...I neglected my aging in place strategy and I'm going to need to get back to it."*

The goal here is to analyze what happened and use it as an opportunity to adapt.

Whenever individuals contemplate change, there is a tendency to equate it with loss; they first think about what is given up, not what is potentially gained. Aging is no different and by definition means change. The SCM can act as a roadmap with guideposts along the way to help navigate the twists and turns of new behaviors associated with remodeling. Aging in place will require adjustments and new ways of living in outdated environments. Knowing where your clients are in the change process can strategically guide your marketing and remodeling interventions.

Patrick, this was great reading!

This was a response I received for a post I wrote on the social media site LinkedIn from a seasoned CAPS remodeler. Jim Costello is managing partner at Affordable Adaptive Solutions and is part of the solution. His experience comes from a place of earned knowledge and business integrity. I share it here to further the point that clients will resist and how a professional deals with that fact.

As someone who has been involved in all types of home modifications for over 25 years, I'm well acquainted with this dynamic, but I never really thought about it in terms of the SCM model (more on the model later in the chapter).

Anyone starting out in this business will quickly learn that many older clients will resist, or even fight against, changes to their normal routine, or to the home they have loved and cared for throughout their lifetime. Some will ask me: "Why in the world would anyone want to struggle up the stairs when a stairlift could make it so much easier and safer?" I have always taught them to recognize that when people (not always seniors) are in the Pre-contemplation, or contemplation stages, all you can do is share what options are available, and, if they are receptive, share some stories about the difference the right adaptations have made for other customers. But, if they are not ready to accept the fact that change would be to their benefit, and the tradeoff is worth the effort and expense, it's time to just leave your card and invite them to call you when they would like to discuss how this might help them.

We have even had cases where concerned adult children, in another city, will instruct us to "just go ahead and make the changes and send me the bill, Mom or Dad doesn't know what is good for them". This never works out, and we will politely refuse the request. Even the best solution is only as good as the person's willingness to use it. I find myself set in my ways about some things, like clinging to older versions of software or smartphone that I'm comfortable with, and indeed, when I'm forced to change (even for my own good), I do get the sense that I'm losing or giving up something.

Building Trust

I think the real key here is patience, you need to take the time to build trust with your older client. If they get the feeling that your end game is to just sell them something, they won't be receptive to anything you have to offer, and you have left them with a bad impression, On the other hand, if you break the ice by solving a real problem that they do acknowledge, (like stepping over the side of a bathtub) without bombarding them with a million other changes you could do, you go a long way toward building trust. This will, more often than not, lead to future calls when THEY decide that the way they are doing things is unsafe, or just too difficult, and they need a little more help.

As business owners, we all know that making repeated trips to a customer's home adds to the cost in the short term, and completing as much as possible at one time is ideal. That sales strategy may work for replacement windows or cable TV contracts, but, that strategy does not apply well to the aging in place market. When you make a business decision to take a longer-range approach and make the relationship the goal rather that the highest value sale on the first visit, you will find that, once an older client decides they can trust you, and your company, to look out for their best interest they will call whenever they need help or advise.

These are also the customers who will tell all their friends and relatives how you listened to them, treated them fairly, and got them what they needed when you promised you would. This may cost a little more in terms of time and effort at the start, but those relationships and word of mouth referrals are worth their weight in gold as time goes on, so, we regard them as not just smart business, but one of the keystones that support our business.

There is so much to unpack in Jim Costello's words of wisdom. I hope you, the reader, learn from his thoughtful response. Jim's approach is caring enough to build a long-term relationship with his clients and do what is right for them—**when they are ready**. These prior four words are the issue and will be the challenge to your success as a CAPS professional.

Larry Hume and Jim Costello both have long earned credibility in the aging-in-place remodeling industry. Their words speak to the challenges of clients resisting their services—even when the need is there.

On Waiting too Long

On occasion I receive a thoughtful post from a visitor to aginginplace.com; this is one of those...**So heartfelt are these thoughts,** I wanted to share them here. This is a compelling story of a caring son whose experience is all too common in this time of life. His is a cautionary tale of perhaps waiting too long—but loving deeply enough to live with the consequences.

Message:

Aging in Place is a fine idea, and I completely support it – until it isn't a good idea, and when it isn't, it may create real problems, especially for our children. I know this from personal experience. My mother was 73 when my dad died. She was strong, healthy, engaged in church and community, and she continued to live – by herself – in the family home. The years went by and she gradually declined physically, but we, her children, did all the things necessary for her to remain in her home – accessible bathroom, grab bars and rails, ramps, help with transportation and shopping, etc....

Now 97, she is still healthy, with some mild memory and balance issues, and still in her own home. But now she needs constant, around the clock care to be dressed, showered, fed, safe and not feel alone at the end. She is too old to move to assisted living – it would likely be the end for her, and it would be against her wishes, which we're not about to do. And as you know, Social Security has in-home caregiver benefits only for skilled nursing, and most seniors simply can't afford to pay for care out of pocket, so that means children take on that responsibility. So, her children have taken on the responsibility for her care – I drive ten hours from my home every other month and stay a month, and my sisters leave their families to help out.

My experience has taught me that there is a window of time during which an Elder can – and should – leave her home for a situation that will provide her the services and support she needs all the way to the end. If we don't move during that window, well, I am living with the consequences. And as much as I love my mother, I'm not about to pass this on to my children.

So, while you are providing us with all the tools for aging in place, I would hope you would use some of our Elder wisdom to address the question of planning for and knowing when it is time to leave our homes, *and what kinds of new arrangements we can create to nurture and support us in our final years. I think Elder owned and staffed group homes - Elders caring for Elders - is an exciting idea, one that leaves Elders in charge of our lives, provides us with companionship, and perhaps most importantly, brings real meaning to our final years, as we help each other in the grand experience of conscious dying.*

Many blessings and thank you for your work.

Charlie L.

It is easier to resist at the beginning than at the end.

- Leonardo da Vinci

Making Home Accessible Before It's Too Late

As CAPS professionals, you can tackle a variety of projects, from adjusting countertops and cabinets to make them easier to access to widening doorways for walkers and wheelchairs.

Aging-in-place project costs can range from a few hundred dollars to tens of thousands, depending on the scope of the project and quality of products used.

"It could be as small as changing outdoor handles from knobs to levers, or changing light

switches and making them lower on the wall," said Suzanne Taylor, vice president of Taylor Made Custom Contracting Inc. in Jarrettsville, Md., as the industry has grown, more products are being designed with a less "institutional" look. Called universal design, these products are designed to be used by anyone and to be more easily incorporated into a home's design."

Moreover, CAPS professionals possess a keen eye for identifying accessibility modifications that conventional remodelers might overlook. For instance, the slope of a wheelchair ramp must adhere to specific ratios to ensure safety. "It's about assessing the situation *and making recommendations that others without CAPS certifi*cation might not recognize," Taylor affirmed. *"The objective is* to maintain functionality while preserving aesthetics. Knowing where to place grab bars or selecting aesthetically pleasing options is crucial. There are numerous elegant grab bars available that don't resemble traditional ones. It's about ensuring the home is livable and retains its resale value."

See Award Winning Remodeling Contractor | Taylor Made Custom Contracting

Tips to Hire a Certified Aging in Place Specialists (share with clients)

- Verify the remodeler has the appropriate license(s) in your state.

- Look for professional designations such as a Certified Aging-in-Place Specialist (CAPS).

- Get at least three written estimates of the work to be done based on a set of plans and specifications.

- Select a professional remodeler with plenty of experience with your type of project.

- Determine how much money you should budget for the project.

- Ask how the remodeling will impact the energy efficiency of your home.

- Communicate your ideas: Explain what updates/repairs you want done to your home. Even rough ideas on paper are better than nothing at all.

- Don't hire anyone who gives you a post office box with no street address or uses only an answering service as a point of contact.

- Never pay the entire cost of your project up front. Base payment on targeted completion dates and make sure your contract contains a termination clause, should the contractor fail to meet expectations.

*Sources: Angie's List and the National Association of Home Builders (nahb.org).

Angie Hicks is the founder of Angie's List, the nation's most trusted resource for local

consumer reviews on everything from home repair to health care. To find out more about Angie Hicks and read features by other Creators Syndicate writers and cartoonists, visit the Creators Syndicate Web page at www.creators.com.

The Consumer Decision Model: Anatomy of Consumer Resis- tance to Aging in Place Remodeling (How to Overcome it)

Words are thinking tools. New word tools can sometimes avoid old confusions.

-Jag Bhalla

Years ago, I presented at the American Society on Aging with a couple of colleagues, the topic was MARKETING AGING IN PLACE IN THE ENTERTAINMENT AGE. I knew many attendees would be coming to the event for the first time (show of hands proved right); and the topic of aging in place might be new to them. So, my goal was to introduce the topic and provide the audience with tools (language) with which to overcome barriers to adoption of aging-in-place home modifications.

This fundamental approach I took was mindful that not all participants knew how to start a conversation with clients or loved ones. And once the dialogue was started, how to further explore areas of resistance to change in the home environment. I introduced the concept of The CONSUMER DECISION MODEL (CDM), which is derived from the Health Belief Model. I will unpack it here and provide an outline, then discuss how it applies to your CAPS remodeling business.

CDM seniors use 4 criteria in deciding whether to accept professional recommendations for CAPS remodeling for aging in place:

Compliance Criteria

1) Susceptibility to the target problem

2) Severity of the problem if the adaptation is not done

3) Likely effectiveness of the adaptation

4) Costs of the proposed adaptation

Unpacked:

1)   Susceptibility: "How likely am I to experience the target concern?"

3 FLAVORS

-Invincible "Never."

Example: Baby Boomer GUY (Peter Pan never going to grow old)

-Moderate "I'm weighing the odds."

Example: Retired RN "Burden of Insight" (she has first-hand experience working with patients)

-Feeling Real Danger "Not if-but when."

Example: Chronic Disease "Frequent Flyer" (individual with multiple chronic conditions)

2)   Severity: How serious does the older person feel the consequences would be if the target concern happens (i.e. fall)?

A)   Medical: Pain—Disability—DEATH

B)   Social: Dependent ADLs—Family life—Social suicide (Have to go into a nursing home?)

"If I did encounter the problem, how important would the consequences be? Would the results be life-threatening? Debilitating? Or merely inconvenient?

3)   Likely effectiveness of the adaptation: How effective the older person perceives the specific

adaptation would be in dealing with the target concern.

"If I adopt and use this adaptation, would it make a difference? Will it do what the professionals tell me it will do? "

4) **Costs of the proposed adaptation:** How costly the older adult perceives the specific adaptation to be.

3 Levels Here:

A) **Financial:** Can I afford it? (Return On Investment)

B) **Social:** Is the adaptation embarrassing to have in my home? (Stigmatizing)

C) **Behavioral:** Does adaptation disrupt my lifestyle? Or affect my self-esteem?

(Biographical disruption / Design for feeling)

Conditions Most Favorable to Consumer Receptivity (Your Perfectly Motivated Client)

-Perceived Susceptibility to the target concern is HIGH

-Perceived Severity of the target concern is HIGH

-Perceived Efficacy of the specific home adaptation/modification is HIGH

-Perceived Costs of the specific home adaptation/modification is LOW

(Note: Dealing with BELIEFS not always OBJECTIVE FACTS)

My Argument: Employ the Compliance Criteria as a Tool! Provides the scaffolding to build a successful Aging in Place game plan:

-Helps Start the conversation / Dialogue (key listening)

-Helps Language the barriers to adoption of home adaptations

-Helps ID specific Concerns & Target Interventions

Take home message: New word tools can sometimes avoid old confusions.

Case Study

"The Architecture of Happiness, "Casa Finale" One Woman's Story of Happily Ever After by Design

Interior Designer M. Robbins Black has seen a dramatic shift in the ways people think about and plan for aging in place. In her experience, clients are first interested in feeling safe and secure at home. They also want to be protected from falls and other hazards of the built environment. Secondly, she notes they desire choices as they plan for the future, which may mean aging in place or downsizing to other housing options. **And thirdly, long for a beautiful living environment that's in their affordable price range.** An additional consideration is an ecological footprint and making smart energy consumption choices with aging-in-place homes.

I Cannot Think About That Now.

Her own seventy-two-year-old friend, who desires a secure home setting for life, told her sons: "I can't think about that now," when they were encouraging her to move from her two- story townhome. Her knees were bad, and stairs were "long and laborious," and a single-level home she could manage, would be a smarter choice. The thought of packing and all the many details to work out was too much to think about, so she put it off. Predictably, she had sequent health problems, fell, and landed in the hospital with rehab for six months.

This elderly woman could not return to her beloved home in its present condition. So, her sons had to add a costly chairlift, replace a heavy sliding glass door, and build a deck in preparation for her return home; all done in a hurried manner while she was still in the hospital. This resulted in undue stress for the family, the elderly woman, as well as overpriced (acute) remodeling that turned out to be more expensive than anyone imagined.

The *"Casa Finale"* Robbins Black decided some years ago, realized that a move from her large inaccessible home was inevitable. The long flight of stairs from the garage was one of the deciding factors. As an interior designer married to an architect, she knew that making the future a part of their current philosophy, in terms of home design, was something that needed to be a priority; so, they set out to find their *"Casa Finale."*

The goal was to find a one-story smaller home near their own neighborhood. Both were committed to using sustainable, green, and accessible features when remodeling. The aesthetics needed to be handsome and functional, with an open floor plan, and easy-to-reach storage.

Bathrooms included a Universal Design sink and vanity at thirty-six inches, a roll-in shower with bench and handheld shower, a shampoo shelf, and a grab bar. Low-flow toilets with non-slam lids and comfort-height toilets (for aging knees and hips) completed the all-important aging-in-place changes.

Natural lighting was a theme throughout the home, with the idea of bringing "the outside in" through additional double- paned windows in the dining room and bedroom. So, as they age and spend more time indoors, they would be provided with a sense of being with nature while inside the ***comfort and safety of home.***

The result, *The Casa Finale* in San Antonio. She believes that good interior design does not need to be expensive or overwhelming and that by following basic design ideas we all can successfully create healthy options for aging in place.

A Case Study: Interior Design for Aging in Place by M. Robbins Black (source)

Original Post: Casa Finale: A Green Renovation in Bel Meade

Summary

The Mattering Scale (Final Key Point to Keep in Mind)

Researchers Rosenberg and McCullough developed something called The General Mattering Scale (GMS). The GMS was developed to assess individuals' feelings that they mattered to other people. For example, using a scale from say, 1 (not at all) to 4 (very much), it could be determined how much others cared. A higher score means a stronger sense of significance to others.

Authentic listeners can push others up that mattering scale where good things happen. We all desire to tell our story and be heard—it's validating and we're more likely to follow through on other's suggestions.

When I am mindful (which is not always—ask my wife), I think to myself, where on the mattering scale (1-4) does this person feel when they talk with me? The GMS can be a useful tool to keep in mind when dealing with others. Not just in personal relationships, but with clients too. If you are an architect designing a universal design home, an interior designer, or a certified aging-in-place specialist doing work for older adults, the act of listening is essential for optimal win-win outcomes. To set yourself apart from the crowd of aging-in-place professionals who will be competing for home modification work, take the time to make this material yours. Commit to being an active listener and authentically interested in the wellbeing of your clients. Over time and with repeated use, the CDM can be your unfair competitive advantage.

Find the deeper story, like with our hypothetical Mrs. Camp- bell, it was more than just costs, it was symbolic meaning that can only be discovered by caring. Listening builds trust and trust builds your business.

(See: THE INCREDIBLE VALUE OF LISTENING TO CLIENTS by

John D. Geddie)

The Planning Fallacy: Tendency to underestimate task- completion times.

Aging in place is a "crisis buy" (put off until the crisis i.e. fall, occurs) because people procrastinate until it's too late. So, if they survive the crisis event (i.e. fall) then, sadly, their receptivity to having home modifications can be at their peak— but DON'T WAIT, IT WILL TAKE LONGER THAN YOU THINK!

What You Do Matters.

Resources

Continuity theory of normal aging states that older adults will usually maintain the same activities, behaviors, personalities, and relationships as they did in their earlier years of life, and they will do this by adapting strategies that are connected to their past experiences. Retrieved February 7, 2015, from http://gerontologist.oxfordjournals.org/content/29/2/183.short

Gravelle, H. (1997). Biographical disruption is used by some authors to describe the changes to self-identity that require redefinition in the face of adversity. In Transitions theory: Middle range and situation specific theories in nursing research and practice. Retrieved February 2, 2015, from https://taskurun.files.wordpress.com/2011/10/transitionstheorymiddlerangeandsituationspecifictheoriesinnursingresearchandpractice.pdf

Health Belief Model: A person's belief in a personal threat of an illness or disease together with a person's belief in the effectiveness of the recommended health behavior or action will predict the likelihood the person will adopt the behavior. Retrieved January 26, 2015, from http://sphweb.bumc.bu.edu/otlt/MPH-Modules/SB/SB721-Models/SB721-Models2.html

Marcus, F. M., & Rosenberg, M. (1987, March). Mattering: Its measurement and significance in everyday life. In *Eastern Sociological Society Meetings*.

Ohta, J. R., & Ohta, M. B. (1997). The elderly consumer's decision to accept or reject home adaptations: Issues and perspectives. In S. Lanspery & J. Hyde (Eds.), Staying put: Adapting the places instead of the people (pp. 79-90). Baywood Publishing.

Prochaska, J., Velicer, W., Rossi, J., Goldstein, M., Marcus, B., Rakowski, W., et al. (1994). Stages of change and decisional balance for 12 problem behaviors. Health Psychology, 13, 39–39.

7

Design Matters

Design is intelligence made visible.

– Alina Wheeler

Myth: Accessible Upgrades are ugly and will make my home look like a hospital.

When I began my journey with the concept of aging in place (early 1990s) this gauntlet of stigma was darn near a deal breaker for most. Gerontophobia (fear of aging) was the undeniable reason remodeling for aging in place just didn't take off.

There were essentially two camps 1) Forced to use 2) No f*ing way you're turning my house into a hospital! With these choices who would want to enter a field where your clients are forced to adopt your services, or outright refused. Trust me, it was a lonely endeavor in the early days.

Don't get me wrong, these two camps still exist and as CAPS aging-in-place remodeling professionals you will be dealing with both. The good news is current design trends have changed dramatically and will make your job much easier.

The Brain on Design

For several years I attended and presented at The American Society on Aging (ASA) conferences. Recurring themes always seemed to emerge and persist throughout the week. One year the mantra was "Design is for all," and a favorite of mine. This to me provided solid evidence for the essential nature of design and aging. Allow me to digress briefly and touch on how design affects the brain and your business.

Each of us has a brain equipped with a tightly bundled group- ing of nerve cells about the size of an apple wedge located from the top of the spinal cord into the middle of the brain. This part of our brain contains about 70% of its estimated 200 billion nerve cells; or a total of 140 billion cells—and is called the Reticular Activating System (RAS).

Your RAS is a hockey goalie to consciousness—the gatekeeper screening the type of information allowed through and filters everything else that you do not pay attention to. And it also homes in on what is important to you. Buy a 1966 Mustang or a new Adison leather large Marielle drawstring shoulder bag, and you begin to magically see them everywhere. Why? Your RAS has now alerted your brain to bring them to your attention.

My RAS for the conference was programmed to "Design" and I was rewarded, because design matters to an aging population and intern your bottom line.

Democratization of design

Much of the discussion focused around "Inclusive Design" or "Universal Design" that will accommodate all users regardless of age or level of physical functioning. More than once, I heard speakers say:

It's not just design for the elderly; good design helps everyone.

Not a new idea, in fact, the barrier-free movement in the 1950s began a process of change in public policies and design practices in response to veterans returning from service with disabilities. The movement has evolved as the democratization of design for all; both in structure and beautiful aesthetics.

<u>**CAPS Chat Tip**</u>
Design's fundamental role is problem solver.

-Fast Company, 2005

"I Can't Die Here It's Too Ugly!"

The late Michael Graves, FAIA, famed designer and professor at Princeton University, became a reluctant expert in medical equipment design when an acute neurological disease left him unable to walk or do much of his self-care. Graves turned this into a best-worst experience of design that functioned better (structure) and delighted the senses (beautiful aesthetics).

Graves was noted to have said while lying on a gurney in the hospital in the throes of his acute illness: "I can't die here it's too ugly." His point speaks directly to the heart and soul of the barriers to adoption of countless others who could have benefitted from accessibility products and remodeling. Hospital –appearing products are off-putting to put it mildly.

Gerontophobia (fear of aging) limited my own mother from using a walker which would have made it possible to ambulate and strengthen her muscles, stimulate her brain with exercise, thus facilitating balance. But the stigma of becoming feeble and aging kept her from using assistive products.

The sad irony is that this kind of stigma which leads to adoption failure, is a "secondary ager" which speeds up the aging process (atrophy).

One innovative company early on understood the relationship between design and stigma for older adults. OMHU (means "with great care") exhibited an empathetic design approach to mobility products.

Worth mentioning here that "Empathetic Design is defined a user-centered approach to product development that focuses on understanding and addressing the emotional and practical needs of users by observing and engaging with them in their natural environment. This method aims to create solutions that deeply resonate with users by prioritizing their experiences and perspectives.

OMHU employed the Empathetic Design philosophy with a nonpatronizing approach to canes. Their designers successfully combined materials from the world of performance; bicycles, hockey sticks, skateboards, and high-performance athletic shoes—and from these made a cane which delights the senses while hinting at performance.

The emphasis was on performance (mobility) not disability. OMHU successfully pulled off not denying the need (after all it is a cane). They understood the underlying philosophy which infused the product was clever in design and used materials which evokes the will to live; a win-win. OMHU as a design experience knew in their deepest intuitions, we all desire a richer non-stigmatizing experience of aging. Now that's empathy made practical by design.

The company was perhaps too ahead of its time in the aging of the population trend and timing is everything. This takes nothing away from design that mattered. So much of success is right place-right time, OMUH created a product that tradition- ally made the user FEEL disabled and infused it with possibility. They employed a second design concept known as "design for feeling. "This approach focuses on creating products that make users feel a certain way, like happy or comforted. It aims to connect with people emotionally, making the experience more personal and enjoyable.

These two design concepts, Empathetic Design and Design for Feeling are concepts you as a CAPS aging in place remodeling professional can use to guide your business philosophy and practice.

Design creates culture. Culture shapes values. Values determine the future.

-Robert L. Peters

This is important because the demographic transition means a future filled with more and more old people. And I for one would like to see more emphasis on matters of design-aesthetics, not as a nicety, but as an essential guiding principle in your CAPS career as an aging in place remodeling professional.

More Design Principles for Your Business

The late Michel Philibert, a French philosopher, and gerontologist, once proposed that we are at the dawn of a new understanding where aging is defined as a pattern of change throughout the entire lifespan.

So, designing for children, older adults, and those with "disabilities" is not thinking about separate groups of users—but a spectrum of human-environment interaction. I call this 'Inclusive Design,' a concept that is informed by the philosophy that living is a dynamic process of change all along the continuum that is life.

CAPS Chat Tip

Aging is a VERB.

~ Patrick Roden PhD CAPS

Communicating through the Senses

I visited Rejuvenation-Portland for the first time several years ago (an upscale chic store that repurposes furniture and industrial hardware). When I entered the store, my heart began to race—like when knocking on the door of a blind date. Beautiful aesthetics have always had that effect on me. My mind went calm as the visual took over and I began to experience a delight of the senses, and I froze in place.

I experienced what has been termed an "aesthetic arrest." This term was first noted by James Joyce in A Portrait of the Artist as a Young man. Joyce purposed the idea and The Mythologist Joseph Campbell in his lectures on Joyce spoke to this phenomenon:

The aesthetic experience is a simple beholding of the object—you experience a radiance. You are held in aesthetic arrest. This radiance, the perception of beauty, is regarded as a communication of the hidden power behind the world, shining through some physical form. This hidden power behind the world, shining through some physical form has many names. what it's called is not important— that you experience it is.

Author Virginia Postrel notes that aesthetics is the way we communicate through the senses. It is the art of creating reactions without words, through the look and feel of people, places, and things. In other words, aesthetics shows rather than tells, delights rather than instructs. The effects are immediate, perceptual, and emotional.

For example, the other day I was driving past the bus stop near my home and glanced over just in time to witness an elderly Russian man with a deeply weathered face smelling a bouquet of Safeway flowers thrust to his nose by a younger woman. It caused me to pause; I felt lifted... it was delightful.

Theorist Ellen Dissanayake defined art (aesthetics) as "Making Special," a behavior designed to be "sensorily and emotion- ally gratifying and more than strictly necessary. Dissanayake thinks that the instinct for "making special" is universal and innate, an aspect of humanity's evolved biological nature.

Even primitive societies with challenges to basic needs, de- sired beauty in their environments; be it for ritual, religious, or pleasure purposes:

For as far back as there are written records, we find evidence of the awe and exhilaration people feel upon seeing or hearing something beautiful. The earliest poems contain loving descriptions of landscapes, of the play of light on water, of the beauty of the human form, of the proportions of man-made structures. The power of music to enthrall the senses is one of the oldest subjects of myth. And, of course, among the earliest traces of human life on earth are innumerable carvings, wall paintings, graffiti, and other decorations, all attesting to humanity's attempts to modify its environment so as to make it more "beautiful."

-Mihaly Csikszentmihalyi and Rick E. Robinson/

The Art of Seeing: An Interpretation of the Aesthetic Encounter (1990)

The Lascaux Caves in SW France are beautiful cave paintings dating back some 17,000 years and evidence of the human desire for aesthetics in environments humans inhabit.

This discussion of aesthetics might seem far-afield and appear to you as irrelevant and lofty—and you may be asking what does this have to do with my CAPS aging in place remodeling career? Enough already, Patrick!!! (smile).

Ok, fair enough, you've made it this far through the nice-to-know stuff, let's get into the practical part of aesthetics where your business is concerned.

Today we are living in the age of Aesthetics, meaning our western culture has become so affluent that our basic needs are covered. Modern manufacturing has solved the problems of lowering costs, making goods/services widely available, functional and energy saving—we have advanced beyond mere function alone. Now our desire for form (aesthetics) is driving demand; and is the differentiator in a crowded marketplace. This has been termed "the aesthetic imperative."

Postrel quotes an influential industrial designer: "Good design is not about the perfect thing anymore, but about helping a lot of different people build their own personal identities. *Form follows emotion* now supplants *form follows function*." This statement dovetails with the previously mentioned Design for Feelings.

Emotion now tells the user what they will find functional. The role of a chair is now beyond a place to sit—it is to make life enjoyable. Think about the implications for your business, this is a whole new way of thinking. Postrel notes that Modernist design once promised efficiency, rationality, and truth; in the age of aesthetics freedom, beauty, and pleasure are now the mantra.

Design's role for aging-in-place remains one of accomplishing a purpose and problem solving; fortunately for those aging in the age of aesthetics, concepts like universal design are now frequently informed by the aesthetic imperative.

CAPS Chat Tip
Turn Obstacles into beauty—or perish.

~ Patrick Roden PhD CAPS

In order for age-friendly product designers and builders to compete and survive in the booming mature marketplace they must design not only for function, but to delight the senses with non-stigmatizing design. Essential is the capacity to understand that humans buy on deep biological emotion (more on this in chapter 10).

Biological Basis for Designing Environments

Durning the 1960's Dr. Marian Diamond of The University of California, Berkeley, did pioneering work in neuroscience demonstrated that environment complexity could stimulate dendrite growth (connections between cells) in the brain, enhancing cognitive function. Her research with rats showed that enriched environments, filled with toys, mazes, and social interaction, led to increased dendritic branching and thicker cerebral cortices. This indicated that the brain is highly plastic and can physically change in response to stimulation.

Her findings revolutionized our understanding of brain development, emphasizing the importance of stimulating and engaging environments for cognitive health and growth. In summary, Diamond's research showed that increasing the complexity of the research rat's environments changed their brain architecture growing more connections between brain cells.

This was astonishing and groundbreaking research because it was conventional wisdom and widely believed the brain stopped developing and that neurogenesis (the growth of new neurons) ceased after early childhood or adolescence (18-20).

Further, in the "Counterclockwise" study, conducted in 1979, psychologist Ellen Langer and her team took a group of elderly men to a retreat designed to resemble the year 1959. The environment was meticulously recreated with period-appropriate decor, music, magazines, and even discussions about past events as if they were current.

Participants were instructed to act as though they were 20 years younger, talking about their younger selves in the present tense and engaging in activities reminiscent of that time. The study aimed to determine whether mentally living in the past could have tangible effects on their physical and cognitive health.

The results were remarkable. The men showed improvements in various measures such as physical strength, dexterity, posture, vision, hearing, and cognitive performance. Many participants also exhibited greater enthusiasm and vitality. The study demonstrated that perceptions of aging could significantly influence physical health and cognitive functioning, suggesting that a positive mindset can play a crucial role in the aging process.

Langer showed how environmental manipulation can affect attitude and biomarkers of aging in favor of longevity.

Building on Diamond's foundational work and Langer's findings, subsequent human studies during the 1990's and early 2000s have further validated these principles. Researchers like Dr. Carl Cotman have explored the benefits of physical exercise on brain health, demonstrating that regular physical activity stimulates the production of brain-derived neurotrophic factor (BDNF), which supports neuron growth and synaptic plasticity. These studies have shown that exercise leads to increased dendritic growth and improved cognitive function, paralleling Diamond's findings on the effects of environmental enrichment. Additionally, human studies on cognitive stimulation and social interaction have consistently shown that engaging in mentally and socially enriching activities can enhance brain structure and function, reduce the risk of cognitive decline, and promote overall cognitive health. This body of research collectively highlights the critical role of enriched environments and active lifestyles in maintaining and improving brain health throughout life.

So, for decades the research is, as they say, "robust" and continues to show that environmental novelty and complexity, along with exercise and social interaction, generally speaking, can support brain development throughout the lifespan well into old age.

On a personal note, I once, many years ago, contacted Dr. Diamond and asked her for some related information. She responded back via email with the kindest outline of her tips for a healthy aging brain. Dr. Marian Diamond identified several key factors crucial for maintaining brain health as we age. These factors include:

Diet: Consuming a balanced diet rich in essential nutrients supports brain function and overall health.

Exercise: Regular physical activity promotes blood flow to the brain, encourages the production of growth factors, and supports neuroplasticity.

Challenge: Engaging in intellectually stimulating activities helps maintain cognitive functions and fosters dendritic growth. **Newness:** Continuously exposing the brain to new experiences and learning opportunities can enhance neuroplasticity. **Love:** Social interactions and strong emotional bonds are vital for mental and emotional well-being, reducing stress and

promoting brain health.

She ended the correspondence with a few kind words of

encouragement. Her advice is worth sharing not only with your clients, but also others in your life.

Don't it always seem to go that you don't know what you've got till it's gone...

~Big Yellow Taxi by Joni Mitchell

Homesickness is the distress caused by being away from home. Its cognitive hallmark is preoccupying thoughts of home and attachment objects. Sufferers typically report a combination of depressive and anxious symptoms, withdrawn behavior and difficulty focusing on topics unrelated to home.

~ Wikipedia

Your client's homes are a multi-sensory experience and because of the law of familiarity, over time they/we stop noticing and our senses are lulled into dullness. They/We become unaware of the many little things which are the scaffolding to our experience of home. Only when we are deprived of "Home" do our senses begin to wake up and recall why we are feeling the loss.

The Senses

Sights: Think about the visuals in your home that delight. What are they? Where are they? The way the afternoon sunlight moves through the kitchen on early spring days. Or the garden light's amber glow in the evening that lights up the pathway to the shed.

Sounds: Think about the windchimes which dance to the evening breeze. What are they? Where are they? Or maybe the neighbor kids playing in their back yard, NPR on the radio in the background, perhaps the grinding of coffee downstairs in the early morning hour.

Smells: Think about the aromas. What are they? Where are they? Fresh ground coffee, toast crisping in the toaster, newly mowed lawn, faint sweetness of laundry tumbling in the dryer, or a fire in the fireplace on a winter night, or the roses in bloom outside the bedroom window.

Textures: Think about the rich sensations which surround you at home. What are they? Where are they? Soft texture underfoot of deep pile living room carpet, or the firm smooth hardwoods in the hallway. Or the feel of porcelain doorknobs in your hand, or the cool solid surface of stone countertops.

Tastes: Think about gustatory delights. What are they? Where are they? Fresh baked cookies just out of the oven, juicy ripe fruits resting in a bowl, cold beer out of the mini fridge in the shop/garage.

Where is your Cozy Spot? Where is your Creative Space?

Where do you Cultivate your own uniqueness?

Where do you get Business done? Where do you Re-energize?

Where do you Hide out?

The Aging in Place Question:

Can your clients Imagine giving these up? Can you?

A useful aging-in-place exercise for your clients is to take stock of their dwellings in terms of how they "Spark Joy" (shout out to Marie). Contemplate how their 5 senses are activated by the place they call home. Have them be mindful and think deeply into how these sensual experiences contribute to Quality of Life—and what it would mean to not have them any longer. These insights can go a long way in motivating their efforts to remain home by choice. Encourage them to do what's needed to continue living in that unique space they cultivated over many years. Start with a Photovoice home assessment evaluation (see

chapter) and follow up with recommendations and a plan.

Get them to mindfully *Just Notice Home—then what they might miss most about not being there. . .*

Design for Feeling

Occasionally a LinkedIn contributor will post something so insightful it has the potential to be a game-changer in your thinking. Todd Smith, CEO of Odessa Connect gifted us with just such a post.

Todd starts out with the familiar FORM (how it looks) vs. FUNCTION (how it works) dichotomy in design, then quickly introduces a third dimension, FEELINGS (how it makes you feel). This is an earthshaking distention. The author notes: "It doesn't matter if the interface looks good, if it makes me feel ignorant."

BINGO! That resonated, because all week I've been dealing with a fraud alert on my bank card—which, if this has ever happened to you, the labyrinth this will take you down for the next few days is hellish. Every business I had associated with that card now had to be reinstated with a new card number. This meant contacting all my accounts and updating payment information.

The matrix of passwords, text verifications, calls on hold, voice trees, ai generated "help" lines, and updates that are endlessly circular and like stringing beads without a knot on the end, are crazy making at best. I really began to doubt my intelligence, then quickly my intelligence—they (designed systems) all made me feel stupid or inept.

More than once, I wanted to walk away from the Gregorian knot I could not seem to untie and escape back to a simpler time before this madness!

Make it simple, but significant.

— Don Draper, fictional character on Mad Men

Simple

Todd confesses "it's hard to make something easy to use" and quotes da Vinci "simplicity is the ultimate sophistication." No truer words have ever been written. He had me at the start, because as I struggled with digital design for efficiency, my feelings went darker and darker towards self-loathing: Like what's wrong with me? When in fact, less-than intuitive interfaces (being kind here) were to blame.

So, his driving mission to keep simplicity at the core of his design philosophy to win over the customer (interface) by engendering good feelings about the self and product, are not lost on me. Ultimately, Todd's goal is to make Form, Function, and Feelings integrate into a system that serves and delights the end user. To those ends I say Bravo! He has my support...

Author's note: When I contacted Todd to applaud him for his LinkedIn Post and that I thought he had the makings for a book, he expressed he would consider it then he "retires." Translation, He's too busy to write about it. Making a meaningful difference in real people's lives is what he's doing. The writing can wait. (See odessaconnect.tv)

Summary

Designing for aging in place goes beyond function; it's about creating spaces that empower older adults without labeling or stigmatizing their needs. Thoughtful design integrates accessibility features subtly, so homes feel natural and inviting rather than clinical. For example, lever door handles, wider doorways, and non-slip flooring can support mobility without standing out as "senior-specific" elements.

At its best, non-stigmatizing design balances practical, safety-enhancing elements with aesthetics that bring joy, promoting interdependence and pride in one's environment. From adjustable lighting that creates a warm ambiance to stylish grab bars that double as decor, these touches make a home both supportive and beautiful, contributing to a positive, affirming experience of aging at home.

What You Do Matters. References

(Philibert, M. in Dimensions of Aging: Readings (eds Hendricks, J. and C.D. Hendricks) 379–394 (Winthrop Publishers, Cambridge, 1979).

Pagnini F, Cavalera C, Volpato E, Comazzi B, Vailati Riboni F, Valota C, Bercovitz K, Molinari E, Banfi P, Phillips D, Langer E. Ageing as a mindset: a study protocol to rejuvenate older adults with a counterclockwise psychological intervention. BMJ Open. 2019 Jul 9;9(7): e030411. doi: 10.1136/bmjopen-2019-030411. PMID: 31289097; PMCID: PMC6615788.

Csikszentmihalyi, M., & Robinson, R. E., *The art of seeing: Toward an interpretative psychology of the visual arts.*

Postrel, V. (2013). *The power of glamour: Longing and the art of visual persuasion.* Simon & Schuster.

Sanders, R. (2017, July 28). *Marian Diamond, known for studies of Einstein's brain, dies at 90: A pioneering neuroscientist, Diamond provided the first evidence that the brain's anatomy changes with experience, establishing the value of mental enrichment throughout life.* [Found; https://news.berkeley.edu/2017/07/28/marian-d iamond-known-for-studies-of-einsteins-brain-dies-at-90/

See
Connecting Science and Design for Aging in Place | Linda Kafka

Linda Kafka Neuro Design Academy

8

Your Ideal Client

The purpose of a business is to create a customer who creates customers.

– Shiv Singh

Aging in Place

Successful aging in place begins in the mind, then in the physical. This has been my mantra for over three decades now. Why is this important? And what does it have to do with you and your aging-in-place remodeling business you might be asking? Just about everything—let me explain.

My professional focus has for some 35 years been on aging in general and aging in place specifically; from which I've always taken a systems approach (theme). Aging in place and ageism are topics that occur in context, that is, they exist in an ecosphere of culture and meaning making—a system.

For example, aging in place is generally thought of in a physical/built environment sense, ramps, rails, non-barrier entrances, single level living, etc., then there are also the caregiving aspects (formal and informal), technological applications, environmental considerations, and financial. However, I would argue there is more to consider beyond the physical.

Any architect worth their salt will tell you buildings (the physical) begin first in the mind (the nonphysical) as an idea. It's my opinion the same applies to successful aging in place, the idea begins in the mind as well. Either the mind of the homeowner eventually, or the network of loved ones who have the idea of them remaining home as they age (whether conceived of as "aging in place" or not). And it is at this nonphysical level of the mind that the pernicious nature of ageism does its damage. The topic of ageism has been on top-of-mind as of late and it is very relevant to your business goals as well.

Margaret Morganroth Gullette advanced the notion that we are aged by culture, and the ironic paradox of a population that is touted as living longer (average life spans have decreased recently) and yet the fear of aging (gerontophobia) is even more widespread and happening at earlier ages in the United States. Our youth obsessed culture sends ageist messages daily. Data drawn from the University of Michigan National Poll on Healthy Aging, with a representative sample of 2,035 U.S. adults ages 50 to 80 found 93% of older adults say they regularly experience at least one form of ageism (10 were cited).

The importance of this concept of being aged by culture is eloquently researched by Yale professor and leading expert on the psychology of successful aging, Dr. Becca Levy. Her book, Breaking the Age Code: How Your Beliefs About Aging Determine How Long and Well You Live (2022), provides tangible evidence of ageism's toll on older adults.

For better or for worse, those mental images that are the product of our cultural diets, whether it's the shows we watch, the things we read, or the jokes we laugh at, become scripts we end up acting out.

~ Becca Levy, Professor of social and behavioral sciences at Yale School of Public Health and of psychology at Yale University

Leavy has found by her research that our biography becomes our biology—in other words how we live determines how we age. And cultural messaging about getting older plays a fundamental role in our physical aging. She showed that health problems thought to be age-related such as memory loss, hearing decline, and cardiovascular events, are also influenced by negative age beliefs. Further, beliefs that are positive about aging can affect health outcomes in favor of extending health and life—7.5 (average) years in fact. Given this fact, it only makes sense that better health outcomes equate to better aging in place outcomes as well.

The Role of Self-Efficacy

Self-efficacy is a gerontological term used to describe a mental state in which the older individual is empowered to function effectively in the world.

Self-efficacy is defined as an individual's belief in their capacity to execute behaviors necessary to produce specific performance attainments.

~ Lee A. Lindquist MD, MPH, MBA, et al., 2022

What we know from the work of researchers like Margaret Morganroth Gullette and Becca Levy, how we internalize aging effects our experience of growing older—positive or negatively.

CAPS Chat Tip
Ageism Will Erode Self-Efficacy it's an Inside Job.

~ Patrick Roden PhD CAPS

Successful aging in place requires a healthy belief in one's capacity to do what is necessary to live in the place of one's choosing. This includes maintaining functional health, accepting inter- dependence, a growth mindset (seeking out new knowledge), resources/finances, embracing technology, and finally meaning making of some kind.

Ageism is a Self-Efficacy killer; it eats at the self-esteem of older adults and creates unnecessary learned helplessness and early institutionalization. This is why I have taken a systems approach to aging in place, emphasizing the role of ageism as the antithetical to remaining home by choice—it begins first in the mind. The cultural messaging is daunting, but the good news is there is a growing body of research and boots on the ground pushing back on the decline narrative.

I'm in good company in this endeavor, the ranks are growing, and I encourage you, the BEST-in-class AIPP to join the Pro- aging campaign for a richer experience of living and aging in place. Call out ageism when encountered and be mindful of it in your business dealings.

Your ideal clients will have a strong sense of self-efficacy, they will be the proactive ones who embrace change (growth mindset) and yet have a realistic view of the limits that can come with aging.

I have often said that to create a positive experience of aging, it's wise to make the future a part of one's current philosophy. Another beautiful example is Anderson Valley Village in Mendocino County. In a newspaper piece by Carole Brodsky, she describes in detail how a community came together in the spirit of the village movement to support aging in place.

The Anderson Valley Village was founded following a book group reading of "Being Mortal: Medicine and What Matters in the End," by Atul Gawande. A frank assessment of aging wisely, the book provided inspiration for one of Mendocino County's newest and most unique nonprofit organizations. "We were so inspired by the book we encouraged others to read it," says Lauren Keating, Village board member. With more than 250 Villages nationwide, the group of Anderson Valley residents began meeting monthly several years ago to discuss and problem-solve the complexities of aging, particularly in a rural setting. The Village's seed concept was to create an organization that helps people age in place.

Gawande's book was the conceptual fulcrum that helped launch the Anderson Valley Village which is a community effort of mutual support. The elements are wonderfully outlined in Brodsky's article, and I wish to reproduce them sequentially here. This is what's possible when the circumstances align just right, which is challenging at best, but worth the effort for these individuals.

The Anatomy of a Village

Step 1

Come Together / Form a Group / Create an Identity

"We formed a group to discuss the book, which we called, 'Preparation for the Rest of Our Lives,'" says Keating. "We brainstormed topics, modeling ourselves after the Village concept, which emphasizes the benefits of staying connected and learning together, as a group."

Step 2

Get Funding / Get Organized / Create a 501c / Write a member handbook

"We received a planning grant from the Community Foundation and used the funds to get organized. We wrote by-laws, became a 501(c)(3), wrote a member handbook."

Step 3

Hire Coordinator

"In 2019, the all-volunteer group hired Anica Williams to be the Village's paid coordinator and accepted membership dues. Today, there are 63 paying members, whose dues provide the income to pay William's salary and ancillary costs."

Step 4

Parce out and identify Skill sets / Vet service providers / solicit volunteer bank

"Anica curates two lists- the first consisting of volunteer care- givers, drivers, and errand runners, and the second a list of people for hire- folks who do yard work, house cleaning, and other tasks. Everyone on the list is vetted by our Board."

Step 5

Focus on Living (not death and decline) / Positive Philosophy as a scaffolding for services

Community > dis-ability

"Some folks say, 'I don't need this yet,' because they're currently independent. We encourage connecting with our community now by joining the group."

Summary

This is just one example of individuals taking charge of their lives, remaining home by choice, and creating a mutually supportive community aging in place. In the gerontological literature, this exemplifies two grand theories of aging; **1) Continuity of Self** (avoiding a biographical disruption by staying in the community where they have lived is a strong part of self- identity) **2) Self-Efficacy** (and inner knowing and agency that you can influence your own outcomes).

Anderson Valley Advertiser by Carole Brodsky / https://theava.com/archives/189044

Note: The Village Movement is yet another form of aging in place. There will be critics, there always are. Ralph Waldo Emerson said, *"Do the thing and you will have the power."*

The Perfect Client

Scott Fulton is the President of the National Aging in Place Council (NAIPC), a teacher, health advocate, and business owner. He wears many hats and is a very busy guy. Scott is also active on LinkedIn and frequently posts on topics related to physical wellness and the built environment.

He recently shared a Facebook post from a person who contacted the NAIPC for help. I share the note here because it contains elements of an ideal client and worth deep introspection for you the AIPP. Scott wrote to me after I read it and made a comment. His thoughtful reply contained these 3 vital words which summed it up:

"No convincing required."

What Scott was alluding to, was this person who provided the testimonial is ready, willing, and able to begin remodeling for aging in place. There was no need to try to "sell" him on the benefits—he was overwhelmingly convinced it was the right thing to do. I can't tell you how rare that is. Less than 4% of housing stock in the U.S. are age-Friendly with a minimum of one non-barrier entrance, 36" wide doorways, and a bedroom/bath on the main floor—that is telling.

The Aging in Place Testimony

I've done more things than most, a credit to my years (I'm aging) and my willingness to invoke change frequently. When I left corporate for the second time, I'd done my homework and entered the aging space with eyes wide open. It was obvious aging in place was a disaster. Even most wealthy retired execs I knew didn't have the answers. The rest of us? We didn't stand a chance.

I'd love to tell you we've turned all that around, but sadly most of still have our heads in the sand and/or egos up our a$$, not even knowing the right questions to ask, let alone have answers that will protect our families from avoidable suffering and pain. Smart people, just naive in this aspect of life.

I found the National Aging in Place Council in the course of my research. It was and remains the only organized group of people with the skills and knowledge to both help educate and serve the over 50 million Americans aging in place.

NAIPC was my fast track to learning and connecting with the community of experts, and those looking to find their niche. It opened doors to a community unlike any I'd worked in for decades, with a level of commitment and integrity I'd never experienced.

This unsolicited account of the value of aging in place remodeling generally, and the NAIPC specifically, deserves unpacking and examining the key elements which place this individual in the "no convincing required" camp.

10 Elements that make up the Ideal Aging in Place Client

1. A positive view of aging: I've done more things than most, a credit to my years (I'm aging) ...

2. Embraces Change: my willingness to invoke change frequently

3. Willingness to end and start again: When I left corporate for the second time

4. Informed and Realistic: I'd done my homework and entered the aging space with eyes wide open

5. Understands the Issue/s: It was obvious aging in place was a disaster

6. Knows Limitations: Even most wealthy retired execs I knew didn't have the answers. The rest of us? We didn't stand a chance.

7. Not Delusional: I'd love to tell you we've turned all that around, but sadly most of still have our heads in the sand and/or egos up our a$$, not even knowing the right questions to ask, let alone have answers that will protect our families from avoidable suffering and pain. Smart people, just naïve in this aspect of life.

8. Self-motivated, anticipated need did the work to find answers: I found the National Aging in Place Council in the course of my research

9. Willingness to learn and reach out to experts: NAIPC was my fast track to learning and connecting with the community of experts

10. Gratefulness: It opened doors to a community unlike any I'd worked in for decades, with a level of commitment and integrity I'd never experienced.

CAPS Chat Tip
Aging is a Cultural Construct, there are 3 Ideologies: 1) Decline 2) Stasis 3) Progress.

~ Patrick Roden PhD CAPS

Ironically, when I go over these 10 elements they overlap with components of "Successful Aging" found in much of the literature on longevity. There are aspects of self-efficacy (doing the research and self-directed), human development, novelty and complexity (growth mindset), building community, non-gerontophobia, gratitude, the embrace of change, self- awareness, and a love of home. **I don't think that is coincidental.**

For those CAPS, OT, PT, UD, architects, and those in the aging- in-place industry, this is such a gift to receive a note like Scott received. It sends two messages, 1) some proactive individuals know the value of what you the AIPP can do and 2) what you do matters.

A Growing Niche Market Segment

Finally, I would like to suggest that you consider marketing to a growing niche of mature single women who are looking to home share. There are three major trends driving this, 1) women living longer after "gray divorce" 2) aging in the suburbs

3) economic necessity.

Gray divorce is defined as a divorce that happens after the age of 50 following a long-term marriage. People over the age of 65 are the only age group with growing divorce rates. In contrast, the divorce rate among adults in their 20s and 30s has declined in recent years.

One 2022 study looking at historical trends in gray divorce found that divorce rates among middle-aged and older adults have increased since 1970. Gray divorce was relatively uncommon in 1970 and grew only modestly until 1990. In 1990, 8.7% of marriages among people over age 50 ended in divorce. By 2019, that number had grown to 36%.

Source: [Gray Divorce: Why Older Couples Are Splitting Up More Often (verywellmind.com)](#)

Older women are more likely to live longer and alone after "Gray Divorce."

Now we live in a world in which adults who are not partnered and are not parents are more likely to live alone than not. For older adults, according to the 2021 Profile of Older Americans, "About 27% (14.7 million) of all older adults living in the community in 2020 lived alone (5 million men, 9.7 million women). The proportion living alone increases with advanced age for both men and women. Among women aged 75 and older, for example, 42% lived alone" (Administration for Community Living, 2021).

- [Making a Golden Girls Home a Reality (asaging.org)](#)

Yes, women are more often the initiators of gray divorce. Statistics indicate that over 60% of gray divorces are initiated by women. This trend reflects several factors, including women seeking personal happiness and fulfillment after years of possi- bly unsatisfying marriages, especially once children have left home and financial independence has been achieved. Many women in this age group now feel more empowered to end marriages that no longer meet their needs ([Psychology Today](#)) ([Kiplinger.com](#)) ([Sacks and Sacks Law – Jacksonville](#)).

CAPS Chat Tip

By 2030, American women are expected to control much of the $30 trillion in financial assets.

~ McKinsey & Company / mckinsey.com

Economic independence, especially among women, significantly influences the increase in late-life divorces. Financial independence

allows individuals to:
- Leave unfulfilling marriages
- Pursue personal goals and interests
- Make decisions about their lives without needing a spouse for financial support

For baby boomer women, this independence has fueled the trend of late-life divorces. With their own income, individuals gain the financial security necessary to prioritize their happiness and well-being, making divorce a viable option for those in unsatisfying marriages.

Most older adults prefer aging in place and remaining in their current homes or traditional communities. These communities were built for GIs returning home from WWII with young families. The communities were built largely to accommodate these growing families: Detached single-family houses; large lots; cheap land; accessible by highways; isolated from commerce and traffic.

The First Suburban Generation

The young children of the WWII generation who grew up in suburbia are now as of January 1st, 2011, turning 65 at a clip of 10,000/day; and will do so for the next 16+ years! And most of this demographic transition will occur in the burbs. In fact, 83% of baby boomers live in either small towns, rural areas, or suburbia (as described earlier).

What was once favored for its "get-away" location from big city metropolis and hassles, now has the potential to be a disaster for aging boomers. The suburbs have been termed **"the architecture of isolation"** by age-friendly city planners for the very same reasons they were appealing to young GIs raising families.

Up front is the location—it's auto-dependent, next is the built environment—its youth dependent. Both conditions are BIG problems offshore brewing for aging boomers who are staying put.

Women, Aging, and Challenges

It's fitting that the nation's first baby boomer is Kathleen Casey-Kirschling, born just a second after midnight on New Year's Day 1946 gave her a title: *The country's first baby boomer.* Fitting because,

although men do get old, women get older, and boomers aging in place in suburbia is mainly a women's issue for longevity reasons.

Women's longevity has its challenges:

1. More likely to be alone in old age
2. 65+ Poverty rates 2Xs higher than males
3. Living longer with chronic diseases at 2.5Xs the rates of Males
4. Lack of informal caregivers
5. Aging in Suburbia = The Architecture of Isolation
6. Economics of being Female (in/out workforce w/family) = Lower Retirement Savings

The GOOD News is Your Female Clients Don't Have to Go it Alone

According to AARP, four million women 50+ live in households with at least 2 females 50+ and are house sharing to meet the challenges of aging in suburbia.

Related to "Gray Divorce" are these data points that drive the economic necessity to shared housing for older women:

While divorce has economic impacts at any age, some considerations that are particularly significant for middle-aged and older adults include:

- **Dividing assets:** This involves splitting up financial re- sources, possessions, and property that have been accumulated over the course of a marriage. This can include the shared home and any savings, investments, pensions, and other personal possessions. Laws about how these assets are divided vary by state, so they may become the source of considerable contention.

- **Retirement savings:** Splitting retirement savings can affect how much each person has available to support themselves during retirement.

- **Healthcare costs:** Gray divorce can also affect healthcare expenses. One spouse may lose access to insurance benefits previously provided by their partner, which can be a significant concern for older adults with increased health concerns.

- **Housing and legal expenses**: Other costs associated with divorce, including housing expenses and legal fees, can add up quickly.

Source: Gray Divorce: Why Older Couples Are Splitting Up More Often (verywellmind.com)

As of recent estimates, Baby Boomer women in the United States control about a third of the country's household financial assets, amounting to approximately $10 trillion. This figure is expected to rise significantly, potentially reaching up to $30 trillion by 2030, as wealth continues to transfer from men to women due to longer female life expectancy and other factors (McKinsey & Company) (Morgan Stanley) (ThinkAdvisor).

This is a growing market niche to pay close attention to, especially for the women CAPS Professionals!

What You Do Matters. Resource

Anderson Valley Advertiser by Carole Brodsky / https://theava.com/archives/189044

Anderson Valley Village/ https://www.andersonvalleyvillage.org/

Lindquist LA, Miller-Winder AP, Schierer A, Murawski A, Opsasnick L, Kim KY, Ramirez-Zohfeld V. Improvement in self-efficacy among older adults aging-in-place during COVID-19. J Am Geriatr Soc. 2022 Nov;70(11):3318-3321. doi: 10.1111/jgs.17946. Epub 2022 Jul 15. PMID: 35838195; PMCID: PMC9349408.

9

Thoughts, Terms, and Tools

Thoughts

Patrick's Aging-in-Place Paradoxes: **Stubborn Independence and Resistance to change leads to dependency.**

Niche Market for the Savvy Aging in Place Professional CAPS

I once wrote about Vacation Homes in resort areas lacking "Visibility," the post is below. I include it here because this could be a profitable Niche Opportunity idea remodeling "Vacation Forever Homes" in resort areas:

Aging in (a fun) Place with Lifespan Design

On a recent trip to a coastal town that is a retirement destination, we noticed not a single house had any consideration of aging-in-place design. This got me thinking about Peter Pan Housing...

Peter Pan Housing

Environmental gerontologists and Certified Aging in Place Specialists (CAPS) remodelers call homes that are designed for young able-bodied people (like most all vacation homes) "Peter Pan Housing." The reason is that most second homes in resort or vacation destinations don't consider growing old when they are designed.

They have hilltops views, stairs to decks, narrow doorways, and barriers to thresholds for entering, and they are often secluded...meaning isolated from services–because they are designed to "get-away-from-it-all! Great for solitude, but not so good for aging bodies if you want to live there in retirement. In an article titled: *Aging U.S. Baby Boomers Face More Dis- ability, researchers report a new pattern of rising disability among pre-retiree baby boomers, the trend showed rising disability levels among those nearing retirement age (ages 55 to 64) and flat trends for those ages 65 to 84.* "Troubling," *is what Martin, who has long tracked disability patterns, called the trends.* "These are the *members of our future older population."*

The numbers may be a bit sobering, but not to fear, if you want to turn that vacation home into your future "forever home" there are steps you can take now to make that happen.

Step 1 Design with a Zero-step Entrance

A zero-step entrance is just like it sounds, there is no barrier to entering the home. No steps, no curbs, no thresholds, no lips, the entryway is flat and flush with the home's interior. This allows a seamless path into the home for wheelchairs, elders, kids, moms with strollers, dads with broken legs on crutches, etc. Any entry will do, front, back, or sides, just so you can get into the dwelling.

This non-barrier entry must have a level landing outside of the door to give room for a walker or wheelchair to rest without rolling away. The entry area should also be covered so that you have protection from the weather as you search for your keys or wait for the door to be answered. Lighting for safety and a bench to put down your belongings while you are opening the door are must-have additions.

In addition, if you are aging-in-place modifying your vacation home to create a zero-step entry, connecting it to your driveway, garage or street parking area helps a person get from their vehicle to the home. And selecting the entry that has the least height difference between the inside and the outside surface will save money and effort.

Step 2 Widen doorways 32-36 inches

Let's start at the bathroom door. Architects design and build a 24" door to the bathroom, which is not age-friendly. The humorist, Erma Bombeck once said: **Sometimes I can't figure designers out. It's as if they flunked human anatomy.** This is so true; wheelchairs need a minimum 32" door for a straight-in approach. If the doorway is in the typical hallway and requires turning a wheelchair, you'll need a 36" door. So, it would be wise to widen the doors now so that in the future your vacation home will be accessible to all who want to visit. Not to mention for you should the need arise.

Try Stone Harbor Hardware, 3.5-inch Swing Clear Offset Door Hinge (Satin Chrome)

Benefits: Accessibility doorways without the remodel.

~ Door swings completely outside of jamb adding width to existing door openings

~ Provides barrier-free access

~ Works on left-hand or right-hand doors by a flipping hinge pin

~ Includes two hinges and matching screws

~ Fits 1 3/8-inch to 1 3/4-inch-thick doors. This is a 3 1/2-inch hinge with a 5/8-inch corner radius.

Step 3 Build a half bath, preferably a full bath, on the main floor that's Universal Design/accessible

A bathroom that's accessible on the main floor is fundamental to any vacation "forever home" (or any home for that matter). With the population aging, a bathroom on the main floor will ensure that your home will be in high demand. The age-friendly aspect of not having to climb stairs to use the restroom will be a tremendous benefit now and into the future.

These 3 inclusive-design modifications are collectively known as "Visitability" because with them anyone can now visit and share your home. Lifespan design elements like these will go a long way towards ensuring a "forever vacation home" will be enjoyed by all for many years to come.

Getting the Work Done / Go to **Certified Aging in Place (CAPS) Remodelers** to find a CAPS remodeler who can do the job. **Additional Resource:** NAIPC National Aging in Place Council

TERMS

Part of the challenge related to pre-planning for aging-in- place is not having a working knowledge of the concept (being literate). As with other aspects of life, understanding the language opens doors to new possibilities. Can you speak the language of remaining home by choice? If not, you can learn it, then teach it to your clients so they can become informed consumers.

With that in mind, here are a few general aging-in-place concepts worth knowing and sharing with clients (and a good place to start).

Aging in Place Literacy

Universal Design Understanding: Knowledge of designing spaces and products with accessibility in mind for people of all ages and abilities.

Home Modification Awareness: Understanding the importance of adapting the home environment to suit the evolving needs of aging individuals.

Accessible Features Recognition: Identifying and implementing features like ramps, grab bars, and wider doorways to enhance home accessibility for seniors.

Aging in Place Technology Familiarity: Awareness and proficiency in using technology solutions that support independent living for seniors, such as medical alert systems and smart home devices.

Retrofitting Expertise: Skills in making adjustments to existing homes to improve safety and accessibility for aging residents.

Barrier-Free Living Knowledge: Understanding the principles of creating environments that facilitate independence and mobility for seniors with disabilities.

Livable Communities Understanding: Awareness of the characteristics of communities that promote healthy, safe, and engaging living environments for seniors.

Inter-Dependent Living Awareness: Knowledge of housing options and services available to support seniors in maintaining their inter-dependence while aging.

Home Care Services Awareness: Understanding the types of assistance and support services available to seniors in their own homes.

Aging in Place Certification Pursuit: Recognition of the importance of specialized training and certification for professionals working to help seniors age in place comfortably and securely.

Environmental Gerontology
Environmental Gerontology Defined

Environmental gerontology is a specialization within gerontology that seeks an understanding and interventions to optimize the relationship between aging persons and their physical and social environments.

The field emerged in the 1930s during the first studies on behavioral and social gerontology. In the 1970s and 1980s, research confirmed the importance of the physical and social environment in understanding the aging population and improved the quality of life in old age. Studies of environmental gerontology indicate that older people prefer to age in their immediate environment, whereas spatial experience and place attachment are important for understanding the process.

Some research indicates that the physical-social environment is related to the longevity and quality of life of the elderly. Precisely, the natural environment (such as natural therapeutic landscapes, therapeutic garden) contributes to active and healthy aging in the place.

~Gerontology, From Wikipedia, the free encyclopedia

The fields of Environmental Psychology and Environmental Gerontology overlap the Non-physical with the physical. Any architect will tell you the built environment begins first in the mind—then in the physical. And like any discipline they too have a privileged code or language of terms employed to convey meaning. I'd like to share some useful terms I've learned in studying both disciplines over the years.

More Terms from Environmental Gerontology

Accessibility Features: Design features and elements that enhance the accessibility and usability of the home for older adults with mobility, sensory, or cognitive impairments.

Age-Friendly Design: Design principles and practices that consider the needs and preferences of older adults, promoting accessibility, safety, and social inclusion in the built environment.

Ageism: Prejudice, discrimination, and stereotypes based on age, leading to negative attitudes and behaviors toward older adults, which can impact their access to resources, opportunities, and quality of life in the community.

Aging in Place: Dynamic, self-determined process of living in a home environment safely and interdependently as you age.

Attention: How people notice their environment.

Built Environment: The man-made physical surroundings, including buildings, streets, transportation systems, and out-door spaces, that impact older adults' mobility, safety, and quality of life.

Community Design: The planning and design of neighborhoods, public spaces, and infrastructure to meet the needs of older adults and promote aging in place.

Coherence: A sense that things hang together.

Complexity: Enough variety to make the environment worth learning about.

Conservation Behavior: The psychology of developing an ecologically sustainable society.

Cultural Competence: Designing environments and services that respect and accommodate the cultural backgrounds, values, beliefs, and preferences of diverse populations, including older adults from different ethnic, racial, and linguistic backgrounds. **Dementia-Friendly Design**: Designing environments and services that support the needs and preferences of individuals living with dementia, including features such as clear signage,

familiar layouts, calming colors, and sensory stimulation.

Environmental Justice: The fair and equitable distribution of environmental resources, benefits, and risks across different population groups, including older adults, to ensure that all individuals have access to a healthy and sustainable living environment.

Environmental Mastery: A sense that one has control over their environment.

Environmental Press: Demands caused by the environment.
Environmental Stress and Coping: Caused by preference fail-ure, prolonged uncertainty, lack of predictability, and stimulus overload.

Home Modifications: Adaptations and changes made to the home environment to accommodate the changing needs and abilities of older adults, such as grab bars, ramps, and widened doorways.

Legibility: One can explore the environment without being lost.

Mysterious: Prospects of gathering more information about an environment.

Neighborhood Walkability: The ease and safety of walking within a neighborhood, influenced by factors such as sidewalk availability, street connectivity, pedestrian crossings, traffic calming measures, and proximity to destinations.

Participation Environments: Citizen involvement in environmental design.

Perception and Cognitive Maps: How people imagine the natural and built environment, stored in the brain as cognitive maps.

Person-Environment Fit: The environment's challenges are readily met by the individual, as abilities match demands.

Preferred Environments: Places people seek out that make them feel competent and confident, where they make sense of and engage with the environment.

Restorative Environments: A place to recover from environmental stresses.

Safety Considerations: Designing homes to minimize fall risks, prevent accidents, and promote overall safety for older adults, including proper lighting, non-slip flooring, and elimination of trip hazards.

Self-efficacy: Inner knowing that one can perform, related to locus of control.

Sense of Place: The emotional and psychological attachment that individuals have to a particular location or environment, influenced by personal experiences, memories, and social connections, contributing to a sense of identity and belonging.

Social Connectedness: The extent to which individuals feel connected to their communities and social networks, influenced by factors such as access to social amenities, opportunities for social interaction, and feelings of belonging and inclusion.

Social Logic: Designed to optimize social interaction.

Supportive Technologies: Integration of assistive technologies and smart home devices to enhance independence, safety, and comfort for older adults living at home.

Therapeutic Landscapes: Outdoor environments designed to promote health, well-being, and healing, incorporating elements such as green spaces, gardens, water features, and natural scenery to reduce stress, enhance mood, and encourage physical activity.

Universal Design: Design principles that aim to create products, environments, and systems that are usable by people of all ages, abilities, and backgrounds without the need for adaptation or specialized design.

Wayfinding: Environmental cues that lead to destination goals.

Get Environmental Gerontology: Making Meaningful Places in Old Age

Video: Professor Sheila Peace/The Environments of Ageing Pdf checklist https://www.aota.org/~/media/Corporate/File s/Practice/Aging/rebuilding-together/RT-Aging-in-Place-Sa fe-at-Home-Checklist.pdf

Age-Friendly Communities: Communities designed to support the aging population by promoting accessibility, social inclusion, and opportunities for engagement.

Home Environments: The physical, social, and cultural aspects of the home that influence the well-being and quality of life of older adults.

By incorporating these additional terms into their understanding of environmental gerontology, remodelers and clients can further enhance their ability to create inclusive, supportive, and age-friendly environments for older adults

Knowing the language of remaining home by choice allows homeowners to understand what to ask for and how to communicate with aging-in-place professionals. Knowledge is not power unless it is Applied; knowing is not sufficient to succeed at aging in place.

TOOLS

10-question quiz designed to assess readiness for aging in place remodeling

1. **Mobility Assessment**: Can you move around your home comfortably and safely without assistance?

   - A) Yes, I can move around without any issues.
   - B) Sometimes I struggle with certain areas or tasks.
   - C) No, I often need assistance to move around my home.

2. **Bathroom Safety**: Are your bathroom fixtures and layout conducive to your safety and ease of use?

   - A) Yes, my bathroom is designed with safety features such as grab bars and non-slip surfaces.
   - B) Some improvements could be made for better safety.
   - C) No, my bathroom is not safe or accessible for me.

3. **Kitchen Accessibility**: Is your kitchen designed to accommodate your needs and preferences for cooking and meal preparation?

   - A) Yes, my kitchen is easy to navigate and use.
   - B) I could benefit from some modifications to make my kitchen more accessible.
   - C) No, my kitchen layout and features hinder my ability to cook or prepare meals.

4. **Home Entrance**: Is your home entrance accessible and easy to navigate, including any steps or thresholds?

   - A) Yes, my entrance is level and easy to access.
   - B) Some adjustments could improve the accessibility of my home entrance.
   - C) No, I have difficulty entering or exiting my home safely.

5. **Emergency Preparedness**: Do you have plans in place for emergencies, such as medical alerts or evacuation routes?

   - A) Yes, I have emergency plans and equipment in place.
   - B) I have some plans but could use additional assistance or resources.

- C) No, I do not have adequate plans or equipment for emergencies.

6. **Bedroom Safety**: Is your bedroom designed with safety features to prevent falls or accidents?

    - A) Yes, my bedroom is equipped with safety measures such as adequate lighting and clear pathways.
    - B) Some improvements could be made to enhance bedroom safety.
    - C) No, my bedroom poses safety risks due to inadequate lighting or clutter.

7. Social Support: Do you have a support network of family, friends, or caregivers who can assist you with daily tasks?

    - A) Yes, I have a strong support network in place.
    - B) I have some support but could use additional assistance.
    - C) No, I lack a reliable support system for assistance.

8. **Fall Risk Assessment**: Have you experienced falls or near falls in your home in the past year?

    - A) No, I have not experienced any falls or near falls.
    - B) I have had a few falls or near falls but no serious injuries.
    - C) Yes, I have experienced falls or near falls resulting in injuries.

9. **Stair Safety**: Do you have stairs in your home, and are they equipped with handrails or other safety features?

    - A) Yes, my stairs are equipped with handrails and are safe to use.
    - B) Some improvements could be made to enhance stair safety.
    - C) No, my stairs pose a safety risk due to lack of handrails or other safety features.

10. **Financial Preparedness**: Are you financially prepared to invest in aging in place modifications or assistive technologies?

- A) Yes, I have budgeted for aging in place modifications and equipment.
- B) I have some financial resources available but may need assistance with financing options.
- C) No, I do not have the financial means to invest in aging in place remodeling.

Scoring:

- Count the number of A, B, and C responses.
- **A Responses** indicate readiness for aging in place remodeling.
- **B Responses** suggests some areas for improvement or modification.
- **C Responses** indicate significant challenges or barriers to aging in place, requiring immediate attention and intervention.

This quiz can help older adults, and their caregivers or professionals assess the readiness for aging in place remodeling and identify areas for improvement to enhance safety, accessibility, and independence in the home environment.

How to score the quiz:

11. **Mobility Assessment:**

- A) Yes: 1 point
- B) Sometimes: 2 points
- C) No: 3 points

12. **Bathroom Safety:**

- A) Yes: 1 point
- B) Some improvements: 2 points
- C) No: 3 points

13. **Kitchen Accessibility:**

- A) Yes: 1 point
- B) Some modifications: 2 points
- C) No: 3 points

14. **Home Entrance:**
    - A) Yes: 1 point
    - B) Some adjustments: 2 points
    - C) No: 3 points
15. **Emergency Preparedness:**
    - A) Yes: 1 point
    - B) Some plans: 2 points
    - C) No: 3 points
16. **Bedroom Safety:**
    - A) Yes: 1 point
    - B) Some improvements: 2 points
    - C) No: 3 points
17. **Social Support:**
    - A) Yes: 1 point
    - B) Some support: 2 points
    - C) No: 3 points
18. **Fall Risk Assessment:**
    - A) No falls: 1 point
    - B) Few falls: 2 points
    - C) Yes, falls: 3 points
19. **Stair Safety:**
    - A) Yes: 1 point
    - B) Some improvements: 2 points
    - C) No: 3 points
20. **Financial Preparedness:**
    - A) Yes: 1 point
    - B) Some resources: 2 points
    - C) No: 3 points

After the participant has responded to all questions, total the points from their answers. The lower the total score, the more prepared they are for aging in place remodeling. Here's a guideline for interpreting the total score:

• 10-20 points: Well-prepared for aging in place remodeling, with minor areas for improvement.

• 21-30 points: Some areas for improvement or modification in the home environment to enhance safety and accessibility.

• 31-40 points: Significant challenges or barriers to aging in place, requiring immediate attention and intervention to address safety and accessibility issues.

Simple 10 Survey Questions: Are You Ready to Start Thinking About Aging in Place?

1. Are you 40 years of age or better?

2. Do you plan on staying in your current home and community for the foreseeable future?

3. Do you or a household member have one or more chronic health conditions such as diabetes or arthritis?

4. Are you finding it more challenging getting in/out of the shower tub or negotiating stairs?

5. Are there steep sloping walkways and/or stairs to enter your home (barriers to entry)?

6. Is your home set up for single-floor living (bedroom, bath, and kitchen on the main floor)?

7. Can the doors accommodate a wheelchair (34" to 42") for you or a visitor?

8. Have you developed a network of helpers ("social capital") in your neighborhood that you would miss if you relocated?

9. How difficult is it to access goods and services from where you now live? Can you walk? Drive a short distance? Or use public transportation?

10. Do you enjoy living where multi-generational contact is possible?

Many have experienced parents struggling to live in a home/community that no longer works for them. Some are now finding out what that is like for themselves. These 10 simple questions are designed to be a starting point in thinking about current living situations while beginning to develop a plan. At aginginplace.com my goal has always been to provide visitors with content created to help increase the odds of remaining home by choice. It may not always be optimal or even possible–but I think it's worth the effort.

~ Patrick Roden PhD RN

PhotoVoice Tool for Aging in Place (review)

Concept: CAPS Secure-Lens is a comprehensive home assessment tool designed for aging in place, incorporating the photovoice concept to capture and address potential challenges and opportunities in each room and space of the home.

Introduction to PhotoVoice

Photovoice is a process by which people can identify, represent, and enhance their community through a specific photographic technique. It entrusts cameras to the hands of people to enable them to act as recorders, and potential catalysts for social action and change, in their own communities. It uses the immediacy of the visual image and accompanying stories to furnish evidence and to promote an effective, participatory means of sharing expertise to create healthful public policy.

The 3 goals of the photovoice method

Goal 1: To enable people to record and reflect their community's strengths and concerns

Goal 2: To promote critical dialogue and knowledge about personal and community issues through large and small group discussions of photographs

Goal 3: To reach policy makers

From the point of view of the photographers

The key function of Photovoice is to give voice to individuals who are the least powerful in society. Often this is due to poverty, race, class, gender, and for our purposes here, older.

Armed with cameras, these individuals can capture aspects of their environment and experiences not accessible to others. The photos, often with captions, are then used to show their lives to the public and policy makers in power. This is done with the intent to help spur change.

Empowering Through Participation

Also known as "participatory photography," Photovoice is often used by marginalized groups (including the so-called *elderly*) to provide insights into how they view their circumstances and their prospects for the future.

The actions taken with the photovoice process; taking photographs and telling stories as they relate to the photographs, are thought to be empowering. And with the feeling of empowerment, community members are likely to possess greater authority to advocate for an improved quality of life for themselves and the members of their communities.

PhotoVoice Applied to Aging in Place Key Features

1. **Room-by-Room Assessment:** Users can conduct a thorough assessment of each room and space in their home, focusing on factors such as accessibility, safety, and us- ability for aging in place.

2. **Photovoice Integration:** The process encourages users to capture photos of specific areas within each room using their iPhone camera. These photos serve as a visual record of potential issues and opportunities for improvement.

3. **Guided Assessment Framework:** CAPS Secure-Lens pro- vides users with a structured framework for assessing key aspects of home safety and accessibility, offering prompts and checklists for each room.

4. **Customizable Categories:** Users can customize assessment categories based on their specific needs and priorities, ensuring a personalized evaluation of their living environment.

5. **Collaborative Input:** Family members, caregivers, or Certified Aging in Place Specialists (CAPS) can participate in the assessment process by providing input and feedback on the photos and observations shared by the user.

6. **Safety Recommendations:** Based on the assessment findings, the process generates personalized safety recom- mendations and modification suggestions for each room, prioritizing improvements that enhance aging in place capabilities.

7. **Remodeling Planner:** Users can create a remodeling plan within the process, outlining proposed modifications, timelines, and estimated costs for addressing identified safety and accessibility concerns.

8. **Resource Library:** Set up a Resource Library on your business website so clients can visit and learn from you. Feature articles, guides, and tutorials on home modifications, assistive devices, caregiver support, and other topics relevant to aging in place.

9. **Accessibility Features:** The process is designed with accessibility in mind, offering features such as adjustable text size, voice commands, and intuitive navigation to accommodate users with varying levels of mobility and vision.

Benefits:

- **Comprehensive Assessment:** Enables users to conduct a detailed assessment of their home's aging in place readiness, covering all aspects of safety, accessibility, and usability.

- **Visual Documentation:** Utilizes the power of photography to provide a visual record of potential hazards and areas for improvement, facilitating clearer communication and decision-making.

- **Collaborative Approach:** Encourages collaboration among users, family members, and professionals, fostering a supportive environment for aging in place planning and implementation.

- **Personalized Recommendations:** Delivers personalized recommendations and remodeling plans tailored to the user's unique needs and preferences, enhancing the effectiveness and relevance of the proposed modifications.

- **Empowerment:** Empowers users to take proactive steps towards creating a safe, comfortable, and supportive home environment that promotes independence and well-being as they age.

CAPS Secure-Lens revolutionizes the aging in place assessment process by combining the power of photovoice with a user- friendly, collaborative approach, ensuring that every aspect of the home is optimized for safety, accessibility, and comfort.

Name: CAPS Secure-Lens

Concept: Assessment is a collaborative tool developed by physical therapists and a CAPS remodeler to evaluate homes for safe aging in place. It covers all areas of the home, including indoor spaces, outdoor areas, and the garage, to ensure comprehensive safety and accessibility for seniors.

Room-by-Room Assessment:

- Living Room/Family Room
- Kitchen
- Dining Room
- Bedrooms
- Bathroom(s)
- Home Office/Study
- Laundry Room
- Hallways
- Stairways

Garage Assessment:

- Entrance and Exit
- Flooring and Lighting
- Storage Areas
- Accessibility of Vehicles

Outdoor Assessment:

- Entry Pathways and Walkways
- Porches and Decks
- Yard and Garden Spaces
- Exterior Lighting and Security

Comprehensive Checklist:

- Accessibility of Entrances and Exits
- Flooring Condition and Slip Resistance
- Lighting Levels and Accessibility of Light Switches
- Clearance Space for Maneuvering Mobility Aids
- Accessibility of Cabinets, Countertops, and Appliances
- Safety of Bathroom Fixtures and Non-Slip Surfaces
- Stability and Handrails on Stairways
- Safety of Garage Entry and Flooring
- Accessibility of Outdoor Spaces and Pathways

Photographic Documentation:

- Users can take photos of specific areas within each room, garage, and outdoor space to document potential hazards, challenges, and areas for improvement.

Functional Assessment:

- Users can evaluate the functionality of key features such as door handles, faucets, switches, and appliances to ensure ease of use for seniors.

Mobility Aid Accessibility:

- Assessment of the accessibility and usability of mobility aids such as walkers, wheelchairs, and canes throughout the home and garage.

Collaborative Input:

- Family members, caregivers, or other stakeholders can provide input and feedback on the assessment findings, contributing to a comprehensive understanding of the home environment.

Professional Consultation:

•   Users have the option to consult with physical therapists and CAPS remodelers directly within the app for expert advice and recommendations on home modifications.

Customizable Recommendations:

•   Based on the assessment results and user input, the app generates personalized recommendations and action plans for improving home safety and accessibility.

Remodeling Planning:

•   Users can create a remodeling plan within the process, outlining proposed modifications, timelines, and estimated costs for implementing recommended changes.

Resource Library on your website:

•   Provide the clients with a list of aging-in-place terms so they can "speak the language."

CAPS Secure-Lens Assessment empowers seniors and their families to make informed decisions about home modifications and improvements to support safe aging in place.

The Process / How It's Done

Most everyone has a smart phone, which is where the CAPS Secure-Lens process starts. The participants include the home- owner, a close friend or loved one (often adult children), and an AIPP (you).

The AIPP explains the process and provides the participants with the assessment handout. The home dwelling senior will take a walking tour throughout the house (interior and exterior spaces) using the handout as a guide and take photos of areas that they see as troublesome or challenging. Then the adult child will do the same and take phone photos of areas they feel are potential hazards for their loved one. Finally, the AIIP does a home assessment by taking phone photos of areas they see as needing attention.

Process Overview:

Individual Home Assessment:

- The older homeowner conducts a walkthrough of their home using the CAPS Secure-Lens Assessment guide, identifying potential safety and accessibility issues.

- Using their phone, they take photos of problem areas in the home to document their observations.

Family Member Assessment:

- The adult child or family member also conducts a walk-through of the home, focusing on areas they perceive as potential problems for their aging loved one.

- They use their phone to take photos of areas they identify as potential safety or accessibility concerns.

Professional CAPS Assessment:

- The Certified Aging in Place Specialist (CAPS) conducts a professional assessment of the home, examining areas that may pose challenges for safety and aging in place.

- Using their phone, they take photos of trouble spots and areas requiring attention.

Collaborative Review:

- The homeowner, family member, and CAPS professional come together to review their assessment findings.

- They go room-by-room, discussing each area of the home and sharing the photos they took to illustrate their observations.

- The group engages in dialogue to identify overlapping concerns and areas of consensus regarding necessary modifications and improvements.

Formulation of Plan:

- Based on the assessment findings and discussions, the group formulates a plan for addressing the identified issues and improvements.

- They prioritize fixes using the 80/20 rule, focusing on the most critical and impactful modifications to start with.
- The plan may include remodeling projects, home modifications, assistive devices, and other interventions to enhance safety and accessibility for aging in place.

This clear and straightforward process ensures that all stake-holders are actively involved in assessing the home, sharing their perspectives, and collaborating to create a tailored plan that addresses the specific needs and priorities of the older homeowner.

Top of Form

"Chinese proverb. One picture is worth ten thousand words."

The adage *"A picture is worth a thousand words"* refers to the notion that a complex idea can be conveyed with just a single still image.

Author notes: There are apps on the market like this, my objective is to not make it too complex by not using one. Most everyone has a smart phone—keep it simple. Ask home dwellers and loved ones to just walk around the house with the home assessment list and take a few photos of areas that are challenging to live with—then you do the same. Come together, show the photos, discuss, and agree on a plan.

What You Do Matters.

10

Conclusion

The journey through this book has been one of discovery, reflection, and empowerment. At its core, the goal has been to equip you with the ideas, concepts, and experiences necessary to confidently market your CAPS Aging in Place Remodeling business. Aging in place isn't just a service; it's a commitment to enhancing lives, fostering independence, and building trust in a deeply personal way.

By blending strategic marketing techniques with empathy and understanding, you can transform your business into a beacon for those seeking solutions for a more dignified and comfortable future. Remember, the heart of your success lies not only in your technical expertise but in your ability to connect with clients on a human level, addressing both their needs and their aspirations. Take these insights as steppingstones to grow your business while contributing meaningfully to the lives of others. Keep innovating, keep caring, and never lose sight of the profound impact your work has on the world around you. After all, your business is about more than remodeling homes; it's about reshaping the future for those who need it most.

What You Do Matters.

Patrick Roden RN PhD CAPS

Epilogue

Dear Reader, if you found this work helpful in any way, I would much appreciate it if you would take a moment to provide a review on Amazon. It lets me know the project was worth the effort, and it helps others to possibly benefit from you doing so.

Thank you, Patrick

About the Author

Patrick is an award-winning nurse. His career spanned over 35 years and included ICU, CCU, Trauma, Inner-city Public Health, YMCA Cardiac Therapy Volunteer, and post-surgical recovery. He holds a Ph.D. Gerontology, MS Adult Education, BSN Nursing, and is a Certified Aging in Place Specialists (CAPS). He is a published author and creator of the website aginginplace.com. Patrick's Motto: Eat < Move + Purpose + Growth Mindset + Sleep + Aging in Place Design x Community = Healthy Aging

Inter-dependence for Life!

You can connect with me on:

https://aginginplace.com

Subscribe to my newsletter:

https://aginginplace.com

Also, by Patrick Roden PhD CAPS

The Senior Real Estate Market Advantage

In **"The Senior Real Estate Market Advantage,"** you'll discover the 10 HIGH-demand features that today's discerning seniors seek in their forever homes. This book reveals key elements that make properties irresistible to these buyers. Filled with ideas this generation wants, and some they don't know exist yet—but once they do, will be highly motivating.

Inside, you'll find:

Insightful Analysis: Understand the desires behind seniors' housing choices and how to align your offerings with their evolving preferences.

Actionable Strategies: Gain practical tips for integrating high- demand features into your properties to meet the expectations of this affluent demographic.

Market Trends: Stay ahead with the latest trends and data on senior housing, equipping you for success in a competitive landscape.

Case Studies: Learn from compelling stories of seniors who have successfully navigated their housing journeys, providing inspiration for both buyers and real estate professionals.

Whether you're a realtor, investor, or senior in the market for forever homes, this comprehensive resource will empower you to make savvy decisions in this booming marketplace.

PREjuvenation Influencers: A Mother's Guide to Helping Daughters Break Free from Anti-Aging Beauty Standards Topics Covered

Understand the Influence: Learn how prejuvenation messaging subtly impacts young girls' perception of beauty and their mental health.

Combat the Fear of Aging: Discover why society's obsession with eternal youth breeds insecurity and how to shift this narrative at home.

Emotional and Psychological Insights: The hidden psycho- logical tolls of beauty standards on developing self-esteem— and how to address them.

Generational Perspectives: Explore how mothers' own beliefs about aging influence their daughters and practical ways to break the cycle.

Fathers' Role: Insights on engaging fathers to promote a balanced, positive view of beauty and aging.

Expert-Backed Guidance: Strategies and advice from psychologists, dermatologists, and sociologists to build resilience and healthy self-images.

Practical Tips for Parents: Media literacy, positive role modeling, and curated social media strategies that protect mental health.

Take the first step toward helping your daughter navigate social media prejuvenation culture so she can define "beauty" on her own terms. **Get your copy today.**

Women, Aging & Myths: 10 Steps to Loving Your Long Life Paperback

You will learn:

- Why it is not about "anti-aging"
- The Grandmother Hypothesis (no need to be a grandmother)
- How to beat bag lady fears
- Why Negative Visualization can support your independence
- What Social Capital is and how to leverage it for longevity
- How decluttering now is an act of love
- Why novelty and complexity should be a daily experience as you age
- A simple technique for reframing aging that will be your new superpower
- The components of a systems approach to healthy aging
- Dreams denied do not have to be, and more . . .

"I had the best year of my life at 80!"

—DeEtte Sauer/U.S. Masters Swimmer

Granddaughter, What I Want You to Know About Aging: A Journal for a Granddaughter from a Grandmother

This journal is guided, meaning it is designed with prompt statements that will get your ideas flowing. There are five sections:

- Lifespan: Life Experience and Aging

- Health span: Health Wellness and Aging

- Soul span: Intangibles of Aging Section: Aging Secrets You've Learned Bonus: Grandmother's Wisdom Shared

You decide where to begin and what to include. The goal for this journey is to enjoy the process. You have so much life experience, both challenging and rewarding, to share. Take your time, leave your inner critic, write like you're writing to a younger self. If an idea comes to you, jot it down, enter it later, there's no order.

Go away for the weekend with a glass of wine or invite others to help in the process. Create at your own pace, let it evolve into a work of personal expression and love. There is plenty of space to add your own sections. Be creative, be honest with yourself, share freely, include your hopes, dreams, accomplishments, as well as regrets, fears, and disappointments. Themes will emerge about your Aging that may surprise, astonish, reaffirm, or even challenge your thinking. Be authentic to wherever the muse leads you.

It is about you—for your granddaughter. That is the gift. This off-line hard copy journal allows you to control the narrative privately.

www.ingramcontent.com/pod-product-compliance
Lightning Source LLC
Chambersburg PA
CBHW071542220526
45469CB00003B/892